STORIES &
OLD YORKSHIRE

Originally edited by William Smith in 1883

Selected & Edited by Dawn Robinson-Walsh

© Published 1993 by PRINTWISE PUBLICATIONS.
47 Bradshaw Road, Tottington, BURY, LANCS, BL8 3PW.

Warehouse and Orders —
Unit 9, Bradley Fold Trading Estate, Radcliffe Moor Road, Bradley Fold, Bolton BL 2 6RT
0204-370753

'Stories and Tales of Old Yorkshire' has been selected from *'Old Yorkshire'* 5 vols. Published about 1882, originally edited by William Smith.

Front cover illustration: Briggate, Leeds, 1800s.

This compilation and edition
© PRINTWISE PUBLICATIONS

Prints and text chosen, researched and edited by Dawn Robinson-Walsh.

ISBN No. 1 872226 91 4

Dedicated to the friends I made at University in Leeds, 1977-80.

Printed and bound by Manchester Free Press,
Unit E3, Longford Trading Estate, Thomas Street, Stretford, Manchester M32 0JT.

NOSTALGIC POSTCARD BOOKS

If you enjoy taking a look at the history of your area then do look out for books of postcards distributed by Printwise Publications

Currently available are:

Postcards of Old Leeds

Postcards of Old Sheffield

Old Postcards of Rural Life

Postcards of Old Halifax

Postcards of Old Bradford

Postcards of Old Huddersfield

Postcards of Old Hull

Old Postcards of Industrial Life

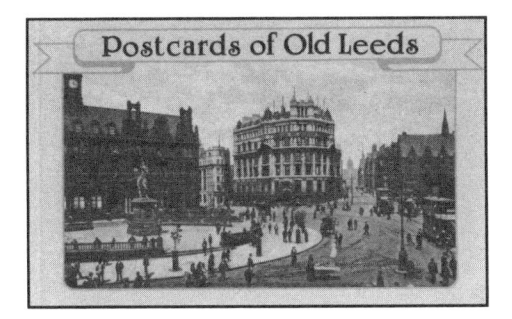

Other titles will be following soon.
30 quality prints in each book for only £3.99

ONE OF THE ORIGINAL TITLE PAGES

OLD YORKSHIRE

Edited by

WILLIAM SMITH, F.S.A.S.,

WITH AN INTRODUCTION

BY FREDERICK ROSS, F.R.H.S., OF LONDON,

AUTHOR OF "CELEBRITIES OF THE YORKSHIRE WOLDS."

"All these things here collected are not mine,
But divers grapes make but one kind of wine,
So I from many learned authors took
The various matters written in this book.
* * * * * * * *
Some things are very good, pick out the best,
Good wits compiled them, and I wrote the rest,
If thou dost buy it, it will quit the cost,
Read it, and all thy labour is not lost."

TAYLOR *(The Water Poet)*.

****

London

H. Adlard sc.

Yours very truly,
William Smith.

From Photograph by Braithwaite, Leeds.

INTRODUCTION

I have for many years been fascinated by Yorkshire, since before my university days which were spent in Leeds. A number of memories of places of beauty and history were stirred as I read through these fascinating stories and tales.

The credit for collecting them must go, not to me, but to William Smith who published in 1883 a five volume collection of Yorkshire miscellany, but written in an enjoyable and understandable format still relevant to us today. The idea of the book was following on from Printwise's successes with collections of tales of old Lancashire, to collect a number of stories in an affordable paperback format enabling people to read some of the tales which form part of their local heritage.

For me, apart from the incredible eccentric characters I have come across in compiling this collection, the most fascinating story has to be that of "Historical Oaks, Elms and Yews" which has finally explained to me the half legends of an ancient oak which I constantly heard talk of in my student days in Headingley.

For those who enjoy being appalled, the tale of "Waterton, the Wanderer" tells of the process of digging out insects (chigoes) from under the toe-nails with a pen-knife in fairly graphic detail and is also a fascinating story.

I hope you will enjoy this collection of tales from the well known such as Mother Shipton, to the more obscure.

CONTENTS

The Rombalds Moor hermit 9
The Nimrod of the North 10
King David 11
The King of the Gipsies 12
The Fiddler on York Minster 13
Yorkshire Local Names 15
Wakefield Races, 1740 18
Foster Powell, Pedestrian 22
Leeds in the Past 24
Quakers' Burial Ground at Oulton 33
A Relic of Antiquity 33
Ducking & Cucking Stools 34
 Wife Sales in Yorkshire 36
Riding the Stang 36
Old Three Laps 37
The Custom of Horn-Blowing 38
Ancient Crosses at Ilkley 39
Two Quaint Church Offices 42
Blind Jack of Knaresborough 43
John Jackson of Woodchurch 47
James Naylor, the Mad Quaker 49
Mother Shipton 53
Historical Oaks, Elms & Yews 59
The largest Oak in Britain 62
Hardraw Force 66
The Plunder of a Yorkshire Battlefield 67
A Yorkshire Parish Coffin 68
The Leeds Civic Sceptre 72
The Ducking Stool at Morley 74
The Flitch of Bacon Oath 75
Horn-Blowing at Ripon 76

The Story of Little John	78
A Yorkshire Highwayman	79
Sandal Castle	80
A Town of Many Names	84
The Life of an English Monastery	84
Longevity in Whitby	91
Henry Jenkins	92
Ancient Customs in Ripon	98
The Halifax Gibbet	99
Observance of Saints' Days	100
The fight at Adwalton Moor	101
A Remarkable Centenarian	105
Longevity in Kirkburton	108
Whitby Abbey	109
Flint Jack	114
Bolling Hall	124
Illustrations of Yorkshire Folk-Lore	129
Nidderdale	133
Popular Rhymes and Proverbs	137
Personal Distinctions & Titles	141
A Celebrated Fair	144
Bishop Blaize Festival	146
Field Kirk Fair	150
Waterton, the Wanderer	151
Jack Hawley	157
Ancient Grave Stones	160
A Breach of Promise Case in the 15th Century	170
Old Yorkshire Proverbs	171
Mount Grace Priory	174
The Devil's Arrow Near Boroughbridge	175
An Ancient East Riding Hospital	177
Witches and Wizards	178

THE ROMBALDS MOOR HERMIT

This remarkable man towards the close of his life lived by begging from town to town. His last journey was from Silsden, at which place he was taken seriously ill. It was thought that some young men

The Rombalds Moor Hermit.

had drugged his beer, in what they would call a lark. The consequence was a violent attack of English cholera. Job with great difficulty got back to Ilkley, and took up his abode in a barn belonging to the Wheat Sheaf Inn. The landlord, afraid that the end of the poor man was near, sent for the parish authorities, who had him removed to the Carlton Workhouse, as he belonged to Burley, near Ilkley. He died in the course of a few days, at the age of 77 years, and was buried in Burley Churchyard. In his time he was subjected to a great deal of cruel and unmerciful practical joking. I once had the curiosity to pay him a visit at his hermitage, and that day some young wicked wretches had set fire to the straw inside the hut, and had destroyed many little things of great consequence to old Job. I shall ever remember how troubled he was, and how he seemed to feel his deplorable situation, and how I, boy as I was, shed tears for the man's position, and out of grief that it was not in my power to chastise the perpetrators of so cruel an outrage. A history of the Rombalds Moor Hermit is given in Baring-Gould's "Yorkshire Oddities." The accompanying engraving of this eccentric character has been kindly lent by Messrs. Thos. Harrison and Sons, of Bingley.

Horton. G. F. L.

THE NIMROD OF THE NORTH

BESWICK, six and a half miles from Beverley, on the road to Scarborough, was the residence of that celebrated Nimrod of the North, Wm. Draper, who bred and hunted the best pack of foxhounds in Europe. He was uncle to Sir Wm. Draper, who conquered the Manillas. Singular in many traits of his character, and amiable in most of them, on an annual income of about £700 he bred up respectably eleven sons and daughters; kept a noble and well-hunted pack of dogs, with horses suitable, besides a carriage for his lady and family. Hospitable he was, in the fullest sense, but without bordering on the profuse. It was remarked of him, that he every month killed a stall-fed ox of his own feeding, and prided himself not only in giving good meats, simply dressed, but served with particular neatness. Few were more rigid in personal economy, or liberal on suitable occasions. Of an aspect and in attire perhaps too negligent, he ridiculed all *fopperies* with strong native humour and effect. His education had been classic, and his memory good; he possessed a laconic manner, and told many stories well. His company therefore in the field and at the hall was much sought by persons of position. With these he obtained an interest, of which he availed himself, to promote his sons, in the army, navy, and church. To the children of his poorer neighbours he was as good as a father. His stables and kennels became academies for huntsmen and grooms, where he maintained— but not in idleness—a number of youths. As these grew fit, he recommended them to other sportsmen, or dismissed them to labour. Many became useful in their proper sphere, and lived to be thankful, after their faithful services, for the rewards of honest and persevering industry.

Mr. Draper's disposition was singularly humane, though hasty, and of a rigid air and aspect. After some few quick emotions, almost everything seemed with him ultimately pardonable except *deliberate murder*—especially of a fox!

At all points a most complete sportsman, he lived and he died on horseback, but not till his 80th year, when, having ridden his favourite old pony as far as Weighton (whither he was invited to review a newly raised pack), he expressed much satisfaction, but on turning homewards dropped suddenly, was just saved from falling, and spoke no more. A singular print of Mr. Draper, done for him when he was 66 years old, was to be seen in almost every fox-hunter's hall for many years after. The family, at his death, sold and divided the estate, which they left with honour, and the neighbourhood full of regret.

Miss Di Draper, daughter of this gentleman, became much noted for her singular indifference towards men and women, and her strong attachment to dogs and horses, inheriting but too large a share of masculine propensity to the pleasures of the chase. A thousand stories are told of her wonderful feats in horsewomanship; yet the most surprising was that she did not break her neck, but died, with whole bones, peaceably on her bed, at York.

Scarborough. T. WALLER.

KING DAVID

THE attention of the country was, in the year 1769, drawn to a circumstance which occurred within the parish of Halifax, and excited much notice, namely, the capture of a gang of coiners, who were apprehended in the Vale of Turvin, a romantic and beautiful spot in the township of Erringden, the scene of their operations, Their practice, which, it seems, they had been carrying on for years, and which they were engaged in at the time of their apprehension, was to diminish the size of guineas by clipping and filing, while the clippings and filings were melted down and re-struck in rude dies resembling Portuguese coins of 36s. and 27s. pieces. They had no screw presses for the purpose, but fixed their dies in heavy blocks. The impression was produced by the stroke of sledgehammers, which were nightly heard on every side, no one daring to interrupt so daring and powerful a gang; indeed the practice had become so common that large undiminished guineas were openly bought by the gang at 22s. a piece. Their illicit proceedings did not escape the notice of Government. Through the instrumentality of Mr. Deighton, a supervisor of excise, acting under the advice of Mr.

Parker, an eminent solicitor in the town of Halifax, some of the gang were brought to justice. At the York Spring and Summer Assizes, 1770, several were arraigned on the charge of high treason, tried and convicted, but only two were executed, viz., James Oldfield, of Warley, and David Hartley, of Erringden; the latter was called "King David" by his fraternity. They had another chief, named David Greenwood, of Hill-top, in Erringden, who was distinguished by the appellation of "Duke of Edinburgh." This man used to provide the cash, sometimes as much as one hundred guineas at a time. At a subsequent assizes he was also tried, condemned, and ordered for execution, but he died in York Castle before the sentence could be carried into effect. There was another indictment against him at the same assizes for a fraud, in obtaining £20 from the widow of David Hartley, under a pretext that he had paid that sum to Mr. Parker, the Crown solicitor at the preceding assizes, as a bribe to get Hartley acquitted. Upwards of forty men were connected with the gang, and they appear to have been a most daring set of villains. Nineteen of them were liberated on entering into recognisances with sureties to appear when called upon. The leniency of the Crown upon this occasion seems to have been misplaced, for it is a fact that the major part of those who were liberated were subsequently convicted of a second offence; and notwithstanding two of that number were then acquitted on account of a flaw in their indictments, before the expiration of four years from their acquittal they were a third time tried and convicted for fresh offences of a similar nature, although their operations were chiefly confined to shillings and half-pence. One of these, named Thomas Greenwood, was a woollen manufacturer, residing in the township of Wadsworth (directly opposite to Erringden). He was usually called "Great Tom," or "Conjuror Tom," from his expertness in coining, which he had carried on for twenty years. The gang used to have an annual supper at Mytholmroyd Bridge, at Michaelmas, called "The Coiners' Feast," The apprehension of the principals in this affair was followed not only by the murder of Mr. Deighton, for which Robert Thomas and Matthew Normanton, of Heptonstall, were tried and hanged in chains on Beacon Hill, Halifax, but of another person also at Heptonstall, who was instrumental in their apprehension.

THE KING OF THE GIPSIES

JAMES BOSVILE was a member of the Bosvile family, of Ravenfield Hall, near Rotherham, and possessed an estate of the value of £200 per annum, at Rossington, near Doncaster, where he was born about the middle of the 17th century, and was described by De la Pryme as "a mad spark, mighty fine and brisk, and keeping company with a great many gentlemen, knights, and esquires." At that time a great number of gipsy families lived on the adjacent moors, in tents and waggons, in whom he took great interest, studying their ways, customs, language, and legends, and frequently travelling and camping with them. In process of time, he came to be recognised by the wandering tribes as a sort of Sovereign, whom they implicitly obeyed and looked up to with reverence and love. Being a man of great integrity of principle, and anxious to promote the welfare of all by whom he was surrounded, he laboured assiduously in the endeavour to restrain their propensity for pilfering, and to advance them in the scale of civilisation generally, and to a certain extent he was successful, for which he earned the grateful thanks of the farmers. He was also much beloved by the villagers of Rossington, to whom, as well as to the gipsies, he administered gratuitous medical advice and physic, and afforded them pecuniary relief as far as his means extended. He was buried in Rossington churchyard in the year 1708-9, and for a long period afterwards it was the custom of the gipsies to pay an annual visit to his grave and perform there certain ceremonies, one of which was the pouring, as a libation, a flagon of hot ale on the turf which covered his remains.

THE FIDDLER ON YORK MINSTER

THE late Mr. William Hargrove, in his celebrated work on the "History and Description of the Ancient City of York," says, in describing the southern entrance of York Minster—"The summit is crowned with neat and elegant turrets, on the centre one of which is the figure of a fiddler." Vol. II., part I., p. 62. As it may be interesting to many to become acquainted with the history of this fiddler, I will attempt to give it in a few words. The celebrated Archbishop Blackburn was a member of Christ Church, Oxford, and having got seven o'clock gates during his first term for "cutting" chapels, ran away from the University, carrying off a fiddle from his tutor's rooms, with which he played his way up to London, where he underwent great hardships for some time. At last he bound himself apprentice on board a Newcastle collier; but in his first voyage to the north, the *Fair Sally* was taken off Scarborough by the privateer schooner *Black Broom*, then commanded by the dreaded Redmond of the Red Hand. When next heard of, some years after, it is as captain of the fearful *Black Broom*, sweeping the seas from Cyprus to Cape Wrath, the terror of every merchant in Europe. He retired from business in the prime of life, and set up as a country gentleman at the foot of the Yorkshire Wolds, changing his name from Muggins to Blackburn—a corruption of Black Broom. Bucolic pursuits he soon found to be uncongenial to his active disposition, so he turned his attention in another direction, entered into holy orders, and passing through the various gradations, seated himself in due time (if my memory serves me right, A.D. 1724) on the archiepiscopal throne of York. The fiddle he had carried off from Cambridge he had never, in all his various mutations of fortune, parted with; and to his credit be it said, shortly after his elevation he returned it to its owner, the Rev. Lawrence Leatherhead, in a case of the most costly and elaborate workmanship, in which was also enclosed his appointment to the Archdeaconry of Holderness. To commemorate his archiepiscopate, he carried this effigy of himself, fiddle in hand, to be placed in the proud position which it has now occupied, through storm and tempest, for so many generations. So much for history. Now that scaffold, mallett, hammer, and chisel are fast approaching him, and the place that now knows him shall soon know him no more—for his downfall is imminent—the question arises, What is to be done with him? It is greatly to be hoped he will find a standing-place in some temple of fame in our own ancient city, there to be preserved as a relic of the past, and that a more appropriate emblem of our Christian salvation will be placed in its stead; for as Mr. Hargrove says, this fiddler is a singular accompaniment for a place of worship, and does not tend to increase the dignified appearance of the sacred edifice. Would it not be a graceful act of our good Dean (who ought to have been a bishop ere this, though we should all be sorry to lose him), with the consent of other parties interested and concerned, to place this interesting and ancient fiddler in some conspicuous place in the Festival Concert-room? In addition to the portrait of him in the dining-room at Bishopthorpe Palace, there are two more—one in Christ Church Hall and another in the Bodleian Library at Oxford. Prior to his receiving the Archbishopric of York he had filled several other important offices, as those of Dean and also Bishop of Exeter, whence he was translated to York, and was also chaplain to Sir Jonathan Trelawney, Bishop of Bristol, one of the seven Bishops sent by James VI. to the Tower. But "The Life of Lancelot Blackburn," whom Walpole styles "the jolly old Archbishop of York," has yet to be written, for there is considerable obscurity existing concerning some portions of his earlier career yet unrevealed, and there seems some little truth in the report that he had once been chaplain on board a privateer. At any rate it seems strange that there should be any obscurity or doubt upon any part of his life, as he flourished in very modern times. There is a lengthy extract appended to "The Corsair," by Lord Byron, from "Noble's Continuation of Granger's Biographical Dictionary" concerning the Archbishop, which concludes by saying "he is allowed to have been a pleasant man; this, however, was turned against him by its being said he gained more hearts than souls." The Archbishop does not seem to have been in any way related to Francis Blackburne, Archdeacon of Cleveland, born at Richmond, in Yorkshire, in 1705, who published anonymously a remarkable book in 1766, and one which attracted considerable attention in its day, called "The Confessional; or, An Inquiry into the Right and Utility of Establishing Confessions of Faith."

York. C. PRIOR.

YORKSHIRE LOCAL NAMES

I purpose, under this head, to confine my remarks to Yorkshire Local Names, or expressions and terms used in the woollen cloth manufacture of this district. Many of these names have become obsolete, partly from the introduction of new machinery and implements of the trade, and also from the invention of new patronymics. The names or terms are mostly confined to Yorkshire, not being common in other parts of the country where the woollen manufacture is carried on. The list is not put forth as complete, nor is any attempt made to settle the derivations of all the words.

Addle, to earn by labour. "Savin's good addlin." "Aah mich can ta addle, lass?"

Bribe, a short length of cloth, cut from the piece on account of being damaged. In other districts it is called a *fent* or *remnant.*

Burl, to pick out knots or other imperfections from the cloth, after it has left the loom.

Bartrees, a warping frame, on which the threads of warp are made into the web. Probably a corruption of bier-trees, a supporting frame.

Beer, a number of threads forming divisions by which the web is made up to the required width or weight.

Cotter, knotted or entangled. When locks of wool are matted fast, or any entanglement of the web takes place, they are said to be "cottered together." Undamped cloth after exposure to rain.

Cold Pig, bales of cloth which have been returned by the merchant as being off shade, late delivery, too narrow or too wide, all meaning one thing, "not wanted."

Cuttle, the layers of cloth in the finished piece. The width of the cuttle varies according to the requirements of the market for which the cloth is intended, but is generally twenty inches.

Creel, a frame in which the warp cops are placed, and from which the threads are drawn to form the web. It is also known as *cratch.* Old Norse, Krila, to plait, to weave together.

Cop and Coppin, the warp from the mule, ready for making into the web. A.-S. *copp,* the head, the top.

Cockles, imperfections in cloth. A "cockley" place is either because of another quality of weft being inadvertently put in, or it is owing to the warp not being properly arranged on the "beam"; in both cases an uneven place is the consequence.

Dead-Horse, to pay for work done beforehand, is to cause the workman to be working upon the "dead-horse."

Doffing, the act of stripping the bobbins or warp cops from the mule.

Fettle, to clean the cards on the scribbling and condensing machinery; an operation requiring great manual dexterity. From Suio-Goth, *fett,* handy, skilful. Old Norse, *fitla,* to move the fingers lightly.

Felled, to finish a web or piece of work. "I've just fell'd my warp."

Fleyck, a defect in weaving. Is also a mining term, and is applied to fissures in the straight beds. Probably a variation of the common word "flaw." German, *fleck,* a spot.

Fudd, the waste from all-wool cloths, being the refuse taken from under the scribbling and condensing machinery.

Flocks, the waste from the milling and finishing machinery, extensively used in the making of paper hangings, and also in the manufacture of union cloths.

Fancy, a part of the scribbling machine. It is covered with cards, and is employed in opening the fibres of wool.

Galley-Bauk, a cross beam, forming part of a hand-loom.

Gig, a machine used in the process of cloth-dressing. One wishful to know the state of trade with any cloth-dressing firm, asks how many "gigs" they run.

Gear, a number of wooden shafts on which worsted or cotton healds are placed, each of the latter having one of the threads of warp passed through the eye of the heald.

Kemps, hair among wool. When finished or "dressed," an end of cloth, if "kempy," displays them to perfection, or rather, to imperfection, for such an end is generally returned as "imperfect."

Kerf, an end of cloth, after being "raised" in the finishing; the wool being left long on the surface of the cloth.

Leyse, the process of interlacing the threads of warp. In Scotland the word is applied to cloth when thrown into proper laps.

Laps, the layers of cloth, when "cuttled" ready for the market.

Listing, a coarse quality of spun yarn or cotton, used for protecting the outer edge of the cloth in weaving and finishing.

Lake, to play, when the mill is standing. N. *leika*. A.-S. *lácan*, to play. N. *leikari*, player.

Mungo, ground rags. Derived from Yorkshire "mun" for must, and "go," the inventor when testing its properties saying that, though it might fail at first, in the end it "mun go."

Milling, the process by which the cloth is fulled or beaten up to the required width.

Moiting, a process by which the wool before passing through the "willey" is cleansed from "moits" or shivs—minute particles of wood and other foreign substances.

Nap, to raise the wool of the cloth and twist it into knots; the smaller the knots the finer the nap. Witneys and pilots are treated with this process.

Peak, or Perch; to "peak" cloth is to pull it over rollers, examining it for damage and imperfections. "It we'ant stand peak."

Red-Rud, red ochre, formerly used for marking the divisions of the web into "strings;" a length of ten feet being "string."

Rig, is when cloth is folded or doubled up and cuttled, then the two extremities are called respectively the "rig" and the "list."

Row, in an end of cloth, is a bar running the breadth of it of a different shade—a different coloured or different quality of weft.

Raddle, a wooden comb, to divide the warp for drying purposes.

Rags, tailors' clippings, and old clothes seamed and prepared for grinding into "mungo."

Raising, a process in cloth finishing, by which the nap of the cloth is raised in the "gig" by means of "teazles."

Scribbling, the first process after the wool has passed through the willey, reducing the material to a filmy state.

Slubbing, the process by which the material is made into cops ready for the "spinner."

Spinning, the process by which the material is drawn to the required length and wound on to bobbins, ready for weaving.

Sizing, the preparing of the woollen warp, by stiffening, for withstanding the weaving process.

Skein, a measure for determining the length to which the material is spun.

Scouring, by means of ley or chemicals, of the cloth after it has left the loom, to remove the grease or other impurities.

Shivs, particles of husk or small refuse in the wool of the sheep.

Shivvy-dan, the waste from under the machines, formerly used as manure, now used by extractors to obtain from it the oil or grease.

Snick-snarls, in a state of entanglement. N. *snara*, to twist. A.-S. *sneare*, a noose.

Swape, the handle of the "jinney" or "billey"; a loose wooden handle, having an iron one within, so as to prevent soreness by friction.

Scray, a table of very low level, upon which goods are piled in warehouses.
Slay, or sley, a small instrument by which a weaver passes the threads of the warp through the reed. S. *slægan*. G. *schlagen*, to strike.
Stocks, ponderous wooden hammers used for fulling or milling the cloth.
Tenters, wooden frames erected for the purpose of stretching and drying cloth during the finishing process. The process is now done principally by tentering machines within the mills.
Thrums, the end of the woollen warp, cut off after the web is woven.
Teasing, the process by which the matted portions of the materials are torn open and separated into small tufts.
Teazle, the ripe head of a thistle plant, used to raise the points from the fibres of cloth.
Types and *Treddles*, parts of a loom, the derivations of the names being very obscure.
Wool, the covering of the sheep, used on account of its staple, to blend with shorter material.
Willey, a coarse-toothed machine to open and disentangle the locks of wool and other materials.
Weaving, one of the principal processes in the manufacture of cloth, by which the warp and weft are made into the piece.
Whartrun, a weight of six pounds, used in weighing and calculating woollen material.

Many other names might be added of a local character, as applied to the woollen manufacture generally, such as bobbins, mule, jenny, porty, blend, wands, &c., &c.; but the above is a fair representation of the numerous terms by which the manufacture is carried on. The derivations would form a very unique chapter in Yorkshire etymology.

Morley, near Leeds.   THE EDITOR.

St. Mary's Parsonage, Morley.

WAKEFIELD RACES, 1740

The county of York is essentially a sporting county. Every class, from the highest to the lowest, glows with an ardent love for the Chace, whatever be the game pursued. No true " Yorkshire Tyke " is complete without his horse, his dog, his gun, and his ferret. He takes the utmost pleasure in hunting deer, fox, hare, otter, or badger; in shooting grouse, partridge, pheasant, snipe, woodcock, and wild duck; in killing rabbits, " Rattens," or any kind of " Varmint."

A passionate love of horses has always been a characteristic of Old Yorkshire. William Camden, writing his " Magna Britannia " in 1590, says of it, " This county is particularly famous for the breed of horses for the saddle, coach, and other better uses. It is commonly thought the best race of English horses are bred here; the gentry delighting in horsemanship, and peasants in the gain arising from them." And again he writes, " The forest of Galtres at present is famous only for a yearly horse race, where the prize for the horse that wins is a little golden Bell. It is hardly credible how great a resort of people there is to these races from all parts, and what great wagers are laid."

The races at Gatherley Moor, which still survive in the meeting at Catterick Bridge, have existed time out of mind, and were celebrated in the Fifteenth Century; and "To bear away the Bell," there, has passed into a proverb well-known in Richmondshire. York Races were in vogue in the reign of King James the First, (who established races at Newmarket, Croydon, and Enfield Chase), and probably earlier. They were at first held on Acomb Moor, now called Hob Moor; were revived in 1709, and held on Clifton Ings, before their final establishment on Knavesmire. King Charles the First was present at York Races in 1633; and Sir Henry Slingsby, of Scriven, Baronet, employed " a Dutchman named Andrew Karne " (perhaps a German named Kahn), to carve in stone a recumbent effigy of his horse,—still preserved at Red House—which " did winne the Plate on Acomb Moore, the King being there." The " History of the Turf " says :—" Oliver Cromwell, with his accustomed sagacity, perceiving the vast benefit derived to the nation by the improvement of its breed of horses, the natural consequence of racing, patronised this already peculiarly national amusement. Mr. Place, whose name, coupled with that of his horse, the famous " White Turk," will live for ever in the memory of all British sportsmen, was Cromwell's Master of the Stud."

Charles the Second was a warm patron of the turf. He re-established the races at Newmarket, which Cromwell had interrupted; he gave a silver cup, worth 100 guineas, to be run for, and introduced much Arabian blood into this country. His Master of the Horse, Sir Christopher Wyvil, Baronet, of Constable Burton, in the North Riding, was sent to the East on a mission to buy horses, and brought back some very beautiful thorough-bred mares, which were henceforth called the "Royal Mares." William the Third frequently visited Newmarket. On the occasion of her visit to Lord Bingley, "Queen Anne gave a Plate of Gold to be run for by horses on Bramham Moor, that she might encourage the breed of horses in this shire," In 1712 she gave "the Queen's Cup" to York Races, and ran her grey gelding "Pepper" for it, without success. Nor did her horse "Mustard" win it next year, but in 30th July, 1714, three days before Her Majesty's death, her bay horse "Star" won the Plate of £40 for aged horses, eleven stone each, four mile heats.

It may be observed that the heats of three miles, with ten stone weight, and the four mile heats, carrying twelve stone, in the Wakefield Races, point to the difference between the weights carried by the horses of Old Yorkshire and those of the present time. The late John Scott, the celebrated Trainer on Langton Wold, of Whitewall, near Malton, thought the present weights should be raised; and his opinion is endorsed by that of the not less experienced and famous Mr. William Day.

It is not easy to ascertain the origin of all the Yorkshire Race Meetings. The earliest notice of Doncaster Races that Mr. Hunter could discover is in the year 1703. Ripon Races were in existence in 1725. Black Hambleton Races flourished from 1715 to 1775. Pontefract Races were established about the year 1800. Kipling Cotes, in the parish of Middleton, in the East Riding, has had races since the year 1618, when £360 was raised by subscription, and securely invested. Races were held on Langton Wold from 1803 to 1862; at Hull till the year 1796; and at Burton Constable from 1836 to 1850. There were private race courses at Brodsworth and Nunnington; and horses were trained at Arras, near Market Weighton, Bramham Moor, Grimthorpe, Hazlewood Hall, Kirkleatham, Moor Monkton, Rise, Sledmere, Stainton-in-Cleveland, Swinton, near Rotherham, Thixendale-on-the-Wolds, Tolston Lodge, near Tadcaster, and many other place. Training establishments, in great and well-deserved repute, still exist at Beverley, Hambleton, Langton Wold, Middleham, and Richmond.

Races are now held at Beverley, Catterick Bridge, Doncaster, Halifax, Leeds, Northallerton, Pontefract, Redcar, Richmond, Ripon, Scarborough, Stockton, Thirsk, and York. Steeple Chases take place at Kipling Cotes, Leeds, Malton, Sancton, Terrington, Wetherby, and York.

Beverley Races were established in 1767, and the Stand was built by means of Silver Tickets. The Grand Stand at York was built in 1754; free admission tickets, in brass, being sold at five pounds each. These were renewed in 1803, but were redeemed in 1854.

With respect to the Founders and Patrons of the Wakefield Races, William Serjeantson was of Hanlith in Craven, married Susanna, daughter and heiress of William Moore, M.D., of Wakefield, and died in 1759, aged 43. Thomas Oates, attorney-at-law, died in 1783.

Cuthbert Constable was owner of Burton Constable in Holderness, and died in 1747. William Osbaldeston, of Hunmanby, near Bridlington, thirty years M.P. for Scarborough, died in 1765, aged 79, Mr. Wilberforce Read was youngest son of Clement Read, of Grimthorpe, by Elizabeth Wilberforce. He was baptised at St. John's, Beverley, 9th October, 1703, and buried April, 1774 at Givendale, having been forty years on the turf. The Duke of Perth was James Drummond, son of James Lord Drummond, who died in 1720 ; son of James Drummond, fourth Earl of Perth, created Duke of Perth by King James the Second, at St. Germains', in 1695 ; he was born in 1707, had the family estates given him 28th August, 1713, was at the battle of Culloden, and died on board ship on his way to France, 13th May, 1746, without issue. His horses ran at York in 1740, 1741, 1743, and in 1742 at Doncaster.

Articles of the Horse Races as it is agreed by the Founders or the majority of them whose names are hereto subscribed for the Plates to be run for upon Wakefield Ings, on Monday the first, and Wednesday the third day of September, in the year of our Lord One thousand seven hundred and forty.

First—Every such Horse, Mare, or Gelding as shall be entered for the fifty pounds to be run for on Monday, the said first day of September, shall not exceed the Age of Five Years the last Grass, and shall carry Ten Stone with Saddle and Bridle, three heats, three miles to each heat.

Item.—Every such Horse, Mare, or Gelding as shall be entered for the fifty pounds to be run for on Wednesday, the third day of September aforesaid, shall carry Twelve stone with Saddle and Bridle, three heats, four miles to each heat.

Item.—If any Horse, Mare, or Gelding that runs for either of the said Plates, shall win the two first Heats, it shall be at the discretion of the Founders or a majority of them then present to give such Horse, Mare, or Gelding the Plate, and the rest shall run for the Stakes. But if three Horses, Mares, or Geldings win each of 'em one heat, then those three only shall run a fourth heat, and he or she that wins the said fourth heat shall have the Plate, the second the Stakes, and a distance this heat shall go for nothing.

Item.—If any person or persons shall run either Horse, Mare, or Gelding for either of the said Plates which is not qualified according to these Articles, And shall win either Plate, or Stakes, or both, such person or persons shall return the said Plate or Stakes to the owner or owners of the next Horse, Mare, or Gelding duly qualified, and shall likewise forfeit one hundred guineas, to be paid to the Founders subscribed towards the Plates to be run for next year.

Item.—Every founder that shall enter any Horse, Mare, or Gelding for either of these plates shall pay over and above his Subscription two Guineas. And all other persons three Guineas, which Monies shall be reckoned Stakes, and go to the second best Horse, Mare, or Gelding, unless Ordered by the Founders to the contrary, who shall declare before the Horses, Mares, or Geldings start, what the Stakes of each Heat shall be.

Item.—No Horse, Mare, or Gelding that shall start for either of the said Plates shall have the benefit of the Stakes unless such Horse, Mare, or Gelding shall run three heats, or shall be otherwise ordered by the Founders then present.

Item.—No person shall have the benefit of entering any Horse, Mare, or Gelding as A Founder, unless such Person shall subscribe one Guinea and pay the same when demanded.

Item.—Every person that enters any Horse, Mare, or Gelding for either of the said Plates shall submit to a Majority of the Founders hereto subscribed, and shall pay to the Clerk of the Articles for every Horse, Mare, or Gelding which shall be so entered the Sum of Ten Shillings and Sixpence, and Two Shillings for every one weighed.

Item.—Every Horse, Mare, or Gelding that shall run for either of the said Plates shall be shown and entered on the day and place appointed at the House of Mr. Wm. Nicholson, at the sign of the Black Swan, in Wakefield aforesaid, between the hours of two and eight in the afternoon.

Item.—Every Horse, Mare, or Gelding that shall run for either of the said Plates shall start between the hours of three and four in the afternoon, and shall have half an hour allowed for rubbing after every heat; And if any Horse, Mare, or Gelding do not come to Start at the time appointed, the Founders then present will Start the rest.

Item.—If any Horse, Mare, or Gelding that shall run for either of the said Plates start before Notice be given by the Clerk of the Articles without coming back and starting with the rest, it shall be judged distanced.

Item.—If any Horse, Mare, or Gelding shall distance all the rest in any of the three heats, the Stakes shall go to the next year's Plate.

Item.—Every Rider shall leave all the Posts on his right hand all round the Course, or shall be judged distanced. The starting Post excepted.

Item.—Every Rider shall weigh before the Tryers after every Heat, and shall shew the colour of his Horse, Mare, or Gelding before he Starts, and shall be allowed, besides Saddle and Bridle, one pound for every Heat.

Item.—If any Rider shall obstruct or hinder another by crossing, jostling, buttocking, holding, striking, or shewing any manner of Foul Play, or what the Founders subscribed, present, and unconcern'd, shall judge so, or shall dismount before he comes to the post to be weigh'd, or takes anything that he has not ridden with, such rider, or the person who he rides for, shall have no benefit of either Plate or Stakes.

Item.—If any disputes or differences shall arise upon account of either of these Plates or Articles, the same shall be referred to the Founders present and unconcern'd, and they, or the major part of them, shall have the power to determine the same, and shall likewise have power to object against any one Horse, Mare, or Gelding entering for either of the said Plates.

Item.—If three or more Horses, Mares, or Geldings do not enter and Start for each of the Plates aforesaid (without it be by consent of the Founders, or a Majority of 'em), then it is declared and agreed to be no Race.

Wm Serjeantson	Fran. Norton
J. Ridsdale	Wm Beatson
Tho. Horne	Willm Naylor
Thos. Norton	Thos. Oates
Ben. Roobuck	Jno. Newham

Sealed and Delivered in the presence of us

Wm Nicholson.
Thos. Ferrand.

The 28th August, 1740, Memorandum. We whose names are subscribed, being Owners or Riders of the Horses, etc., that are entered according to the Within Articles, Do, upon hearing the same Articles read, agree to the same.

Witness to the signing hereof,

Thos. Ferrand.
Thomas Furby, For Mr. Cuthbert Constable.
Wm Marriner, For Mr. Josuah Walters.
John Jackson, For Mr. Thomas Lawson.
Michael Todd, For the Duke of Perth.
William Auston, For Wm Osbaldeston, Esq.
Wills Dangon. John Hareson, For Wm Harvey. John Singleton, For Mr. Reed.

Langton Hall, May, 1884.   CHARLES BEST NORCLIFFE, M.A.

FOSTER POWELL, THE PEDESTRIAN

THIS celebrated pedestrian was born in 1734, at Horsforth, near Leeds, in Yorkshire. In 1762, he went to London, and articled himself to an attorney in the Temple. After the expiration of his clerkship, he remained with his uncle, Mr. Powell, of the New Inn, and when he died engaged himself with a Mr. Stokes, and after his decease with a Mr. Bingley, both of the same place. Before his engagement with Stokes he undertook, in the year 1764, not for any wager, to walk fifty miles on the Bath road in seven hours, which he accomplished in the time, having gone the first ten miles in one hour, although encumbered in a great coat and leather breeches. He visited several parts of Switzerland and France, and gained much praise there for his pedestrianism; but in the year 1773, he walked from London to York and back again, a distance of 400 miles, in 5 days and 18 hours. This was his first match for a wager. In November, 1778, he attempted to run two miles in ten minutes for a wager. He started from Lea Bridge and lost it only by half-a-minute. In 1786, he undertook to walk a hundred miles on the Bath road in twenty-four hours—fifty miles out and fifty miles in. He completed this journey three-quarters of an hour within the time agreed on. In 1787 he undertook to walk from Canterbury to London Bridge and back again in twenty-four hours, the distance being twelve miles more than his former journey. This he accomplished to the astonishment of thousands of anxious spectators who were assembled to witness the completion of his task. The following year, 1788, he engaged to go his favourite journey from London to York and back again in six days, which he executed in five days twenty hours. After this he did not undertake any journey till the year 1790, when he set off to walk from London to York and back again in six days, but which he accomplished in five days eighteen hours. In 1792, he determined to repeat his journey to York and back again, for the last time in his life, and convince the world he could do it in a shorter time than ever he had, though now at the advanced age of 58 years. Accordingly he set out from Shoreditch Church to York Minster and back again, which he completed in five days fifteen and a quarter hours. On his return he was saluted with the loud huzzas of the astonished and anxious spectators. In the same year he walked, for a bet of twenty guineas, six miles in fifty-five and a half minutes on the Clapham-road. Shortly afterwards he went down to Brighthelmstone, and engaged to walk one mile and run another in fifteen minutes; he walked the mile in nine minutes and twenty-three seconds, and ran the other mile in five minutes and twenty seconds, by which he was seventeen seconds less than the time allowed him. Previous to this he undertook a journey to Canterbury, but by unfortunately mistaking the road from Blackheath to London, he unavoidably lost the wager; yet he gained more money by this accident than all the journeys he accomplished, for his friends, feeling for the great disappointment he experienced, made a subscription and collected for him a good present. Powell despised wealth, and notwithstanding his many opportunities of acquiring money, £10 was the largest sum he ever made, which was at the time of the before-mentioned subscription. He was always content with a little for himself, and happy in winning much for others. He seems to have considered his wonderful agility as a circumstance from which he derived great glory. In person he was tall and thin, about five feet nine inches high, very strong downwards, well calculated for walking, and rather of a sallow complexion, in disposition he was mild and gentle and possessed many valuable qualifications. In diet he was somewhat particular, as he preferred light food; he abstained from liquors; but on his journey made use of brandy, and when travelling the delay he met with at the inns, for he had particular hours for taking refreshment, often chagrined him. No wonder indeed if on this account he had often lost his wagers. He allowed himself but five hours' rest, which took place from eleven o'clock at night. In 1793 he was suddenly taken ill, and died on the 15th of April, at his apartments at New Inn, in rather indigent circumstances, for, notwithstanding his wonderful feats, and the means he had of attaining wealth, poverty was the constant companion of his travels through life, even to the hour of his death. The faculty attributed the cause of his sudden dissolution to the great exertion of his last journey to York, for being determined to complete it in less time than ever, he probably exceeded and forced his strength. On the afternoon of the 22nd his remains were brought, according to his own request, to the burying ground of St. Faith, St. Paul's Churchyard. The funeral was characteristically a *walking* one, from New Inn, through Fleet-street, and up Ludgate-hill. The followers were twenty, on foot, in black gowns, and after them came three mourning coaches. The attendants were all men of respectability. The ceremony was conducted with much decency, and a very great concourse of people attended, He was buried near the only tree in the churchyard. His age, which was 59 years, was inscribed on his coffin."

Woodhouse. A. H.

LEEDS IN THE PAST

LEEDS is one of the great industrial capitals of Yorkshire and the North of England. Its origin and early history are wrapt in complete obscurity, and we will not attempt to unravel the mystery attaching to the district of *Loidis*, mentioned by Bede, the problematical kingdom of *Elmete*, which is said to have comprised the western portion of *Loidis*, or the locality over which "Cerdic, King of Britons," ruled. If not on the site of a Roman station, Leeds was probably in the immediate vicinity of Roman settlements, and more than one Roman road probably passed through or near it. Heaps of *scoriæ* have been found here, and it is not improbable that Leeds was the site of one of the ironworks established by the Romans in this district. In "Domesday Survey" it appears as part of the possessions of Ilbert de Lacy, under the name of *Ledes*. This baron is said to have built a castle here, on Mill Hill, on the north side of the town, which was besieged and taken by King Stephen in 1139; and here Richard II. was confined for a short time; but all trace of it had disappeared in the reign of Henry VIII. Ilbert de Laci had here ten carucates and six oxgangs of taxable land, as much of which was arable as could be tilled with six ploughs. There were in the whole district twenty-seven *villani*, and four sochmen with fourteen ploughs, a church and a mill, and ten acres of meadow, of which £7 4s. was the estimated value. A charter is quoted by Whitaker from an incorrect copy, by which, in the ninth of John, Maurice Paganel grants certain privileges to his burgesses of Ledes, from which it would seem to have become by that time a considerable town for those days.

Arms of Lacy.

Leeds is situated twenty-four miles south-west from York, on both sides of the river Aire, the principal and best part standing on the slope of a hill, north of that river, and the buildings covering a space of about 1,000 acres. The largest part of the town is irregularly built, with narrow and crooked streets, but the centre and west end comprise several handsome streets, lined with fine houses. The situation of the town must have always recommended it as a place of traffic and business, and its natural advantages have been improved to the utmost. It stands in a fertile country, intersected with rivers, and possessing rich beds of coal. It communicates with the Humber and the German Ocean by means of the Aire and Calder Navigation, which allows vessels of 120 tons to come up to the town. On the other hand, it communicates with the Mersey and Liverpool by the Leeds and Liverpool Canal, and it has now railway communication with the principal towns in the kingdom. Its rise, however, to its present state of importance and prosperity is comparatively of recent date. It probably was a seat of the cloth trade from an early period, perhaps from the settlement of the Flemings in Yorkshire, in the time of Edward III.; but we have no special notice of it before the time of Henry VIII., when Leland describes it as "a pretty market town subsisting chiefly by clothing, reasonably well built, and as large as Bradford, but not so 'quick' as it, and considerably less in size than Wakefield." In 1642 it was taken by the Cavaliers, under the Marquis of Newcastle, and in the following year retaken by Sir Thomas Fairfax, after a severe struggle, 500 prisoners remaining in his hands. At the beginning of the last century the town had become the great centre of the woollen cloth trade.

De Foe, writing about the year 1714, says that the cloths made here are called in London "narrow," by way of distinction from the "broad" cloths of Wilts, Gloucestershire, Somerset, and Devon. He speaks in the highest terms of admiration of the noble scene of industry and application which, joined to its market, brought many "travellers and gentlemen from Hamburgh, and even from Leipsic, in Saxony, on purpose to see it." The cloth market was at first held on the large and wide bridge that crossed the Aire, afterwards in the street now called Briggate, until in 1758 the Mixed Cloth Hall was built, and in 1775 the White Cloth Hall, which has since been rebuilt.

The prosperity of the town increased gradually, though steadily, till the beginning of the present century, when, like other manufacturing

White Cloth Hall, Leeds.

towns in the north, it made sudden and rapid progress, the population rising from 53,162, in 1801, to 310,000 in 1881.

Such was the rapid growth of the woollen cloth trade in the town of Leeds and the neighbourhood, in the eighteenth century, that in 1772 the surprising number of 210,119 pieces of broad and narrow cloth were sold at Leeds. And in 1776 the report of woollens manufactured in the West Riding, states that the following were produced from Easter, 1775, to Easter, 1776, viz:—Of narrow cloth 99,586, and of broad cloth 99,773 pieces, being an increase of 6,687 pieces above the previous year. A subsequent report states that from the 25th of March, 1780, to the same date, 1781, there were made in the West Riding 98,721 pieces of narrow, and 102,018 pieces of broad cloth, being an increase in the former of 11,412, and in the latter of 7,393 pieces above the quantity made the year before. Towards the close of the eighteenth century, many complaints arose from the manufacturers of Yorkshire and elsewhere, concerning the export of wool. Several prohibitory enactments where passed by the Legislature, and much smuggling and contraband traffic followed. In 1788 three Swedish ships were seized in the port of Hull, for smuggling wool out of the kingdom, and it was asserted that, for several years, they had taken out thirteen hundred packs annually. On July first, of the same year, great rejoicings were held at Leeds, and a grand procession of the woollen operatives followed, as a demonstration of their gratitude to Parliament for the passing of the bill to prevent the exportation of live sheep and wool, in which the French had encouraged an illicit trade, for the purpose of robbing the English clothier of his staple.

In Arthur Young's "Annals of Agriculture," a curious picture is given of the state of machinery in the woollen mills at Leeds, in 1796. Great improvements had previously been effected in the steam-engine by James Watt, by means of which a superior mechanical and economic power was obtained for driving machinery in mills. Young informs us that in that year Leeds had six or seven steam-engines for mills, and one for a dyeing-house. Spinners in Leeds earned about tenpence per day, and some of them a shilling. Croppers, shearmen, and knappers earned from a guinea to thirty shillings per week, and he adds, " the machines which have done so much for the cotton trade," alluding no doubt to the inventions by Hargreaves, Arkwright, and Crompton, "are fast introducing here." At this period, weavers in cottages earned generally twelve shillings a week, and some of them as low as nine shillings.

Ralph Thoresby, the distinguished historian of Leeds, who lived through so eventful a period in our national history, from the great rebellion to the accession of the House of Hanover, tells us, in his *Ducatus Leodiensis,* that the 'district round Leeds and Haslewood formed that portion of Yorkshire which Bishop Tunstall showed to King Henry the Eighth, in his royal progress to York in 1548, and which he avowed to be the richest he ever found in all his travels through Europe. The name Leeds is said to be a corruption of Loidis, from Loidi, the name of the Saxon proprietor. In Saxon times it was held of the crown by seven Thanes, and this Loidi was probably the chief of them. It was granted by the conqueror to Ilbert de Laci, as part of the barony of Pontefract. Leeds consisted then of Briggate, Kirkgate, and Swinegate; nor was the private residence of the tradesman disassociated from the place and scene of his business; while the power of the feudal lord was embodied in the castle that stood in the rear of the town. That castle, held by the Paganels under the great house of Laci, occupied the site at present surrounded by Mill Hill, Bishopgate, and the western part of Boar Lane. It was, in all probability, circled by a moat and an extensive park, as we may gather from the names Park Row, Park Square, Park Place, Park Lane, and

Briggate.

Park House. From the remains discovered in 1836, it appears that the castle had a semi-circular form, and that it terminated in the Mill Goit. On his march against the Scotch, that impersonation of Norman chivalry, Stephen of Blois, besieged this stronghold and took it. Here too within its gloomy walls the ill-starred son of the hero of Crecy was detained on his way to Pontefract, where Richard the Second was to end his days by the assassin's hand. Well, but quaintly, does the old chronicler describe the last pilgrimage of him whom Shakspeare makes Henry of Bolingbroke style his " fear " :—

> The Kyng then sent, Kyng Richard to Ledis,
> There to be kept surely in privitee ;
> Fro thens after to Pyckering went he needis,
> And to Knaresbro' after led was he ;
> But to Pomfret last, where he did dee.

Briggate, obviously the bridge gate, (the bridge dating back from Edward the Third, the patron and founder of the English woollen trade,) was formerly, even up to 1825, divided by a central row of shops and houses known as Middle Row. Here stood the Moot Hall, decorated in Thoresby's days by that statue of "good Queen Anne," which is now in the Town Hall. The prison, the stocks, and the town cross were here ; and here, at the " Brig-end Shots" the clothiers refreshed their inner man with a pot of ale, a noggin of porridge, and a trencher of boiled or roast meat for two pence, at which magnificent rate Thoresby informs us that he feasted a couple of archdeacons. In Kirkgate—this name too tells its own story,—has stood from time immemorial the Parish Church, the Church of St. Peter. It is the opinion of the antiquarian Whitaker, that the original Saxon church had been superseded by a Norman one, of which in his day no trace remained ; the nave and transept being third pointed or decorated, and the rest of the church of the debased perpendicular of the reigns of the Seventh and Eighth Henry. Of that church not a wreck remains. The advowson of this benefice was granted by Ralph Paganel to the Priory of the Holy Trinity, York, in 1089, in whose hands it remained until the dissolution, when it was made over by letters patent of Henry the Eighth to one Thomas Culpepper. It came into the hands of the present patrons by purchase made by the town, and which was confirmed by a decision of the great Lord Bacon. Of the vicars before the Reformation, the only name worthy of special mention is that of John France, the exiled Bishop of Ross, for by a somewhat curious coincidence there was present at the consecration of the present church in 1841 the Bishop of Moray and Ross. Of the vicars after the Reformation, the most distinguished were Robinson and Lake. The former, sister's son of John Harrison, was the victim of Puritan persecution, and had to fly for his life when Fairfax besieged and took Leeds. He was altogether a most unfortunate person, for he only escaped the clutches of Laud to fall into those of the Roundheads. Accused to the Archbishop of heterodoxy for preaching on the text, "Keep yourselves from idols," he was no sooner acquitted of this charge than he was ejected and imprisoned by order of the Parliament. In his place was intruded one Peter Saxton, a Bramley man, of the straitest sect of Puritanism. Of Lake, it may be mentioned that he was successively Bishop of Sodor and Man, Bristol, and Chichester. He was one of the famous seven bishops sent to the Tower, and afterwards a non-juror. Where now stands the Covered Market there stood until recently the second vicarage. In Kirkgate, too, Thoresby was born, one of the Fairfax family resided who wrote on Demonology, and hither to the public bakehouse, a manorial right, like the King's Mills, the good folk brought their bread. Boar Lane, or as it ought to be written Bore, being a corruption of Burgus, *i.e.*, the mediæval Latin for castrum, a camp, derived its name from its proximity to the castle; there in the Charles' days the gentry of the town had their summer residences pleasantly overlooking "the delicatest flood" of Aire, in Celtic tongue the bright—alas! no longer the bright. On the east side of this street stood John Harrison's villa, which had one thing very peculiar in it, viz., holes or passages cut in the doors and ceilings for the free passage of cats, for which animals he seems to have had as great an affection as another great benefactor, Dick Whittington. Trinity Church dates from 1722. Thoresby thus writes in his diary:— "August 27th. After an anthem sung by the charity children at the Parish Church, the mayor and aldermen, with the clergy and gentry, went in procession to the Burrow Lane, where Parson Robinson laid the first stone of the new church, (and three guineas under it for the workmen); there was great rejoicing, and if the loud huzza seemed carnal to some, there was, I question not, much spiritual rejoicing in others." The following facts tell forcibly the changes that time has wrought:—The Calls were so called from the Latin Callis. a path, because there in the country were flowery pathways. In Swinegate swine were washed. In Lowerhead Row was the pig market. In Upperhead Row the horse fair. At Sheepscar the sheep were scoured, and at Buslingthorpe the oxen grazed. Cavalier Hill points out the great civil war, when the Marquis of Newcastle overawed, from this commanding position, the town by his famous white-coated Lambs. Wade House and Wade Lane recall the memory of that road-making Marshal Wade, as Camp Road does of his army, where, as the chronicle says, in the famous '45, " in December, for two nights, about 13,000 of the King's foot, with 20 pieces of brass cannon, encamped in the town on the west side of Sheepscar Lane, English, Dutch, and Swiss." But enough of localities. Pass we on to the history of Leeds as a corporate body. Honoured be the name of Maurice Paganel! He it was who first raised his villeins of Leeds into free burgesses. Imitating the example of his superior Lord Roger de Laci, who before had granted the like immunities in his barony of Pontefract, he made Leeds what it now is, a free town. In the 9th year of the reign of King John both the greater and the lesser barons figure as the assertors of the rights of Englishmen in that palladium of English freedom—Magna Charta; both paid the penalty of liberators by forfeiture to the Crown. Now Leeds falls to the house of Lancaster by marriage. Then it was that John of Gaunt—Shakspeare's time-honoured Lancaster—killed with his own hand, not far from where All Saints' Church now stands on the York Road, the last wolf seen in these northern parts. Henry of Bolingbroke, by his accession to the throne, elevated Leeds to the rank of a royal barony, until, by the demise of Anne of Denmark, part of whose jointure it was, it passed by sale into private hands. To Charles the First the town owes its first charter. The golden fleece in the Coat tells its own story, signifying, of course, the staple manufacture of this town, and once of this island. The owls commemorate the first alderman, Sir John Savile, and the white mullets on the sable chief the first Mayor of the Danby family; and the motto, "For the King and the law," testifies the tried loyalty of this ancient town.

Arms of Savile.

Leeds still possesses that very newspaper, the *Leeds Mercury*, which was founded there, the first of its class, above a century and a half ago, A.D. 1718. Fourscore years elapsed before it grew into eminence in the hands of Mr. Baines, who has been called the "Leeds Walter." In the first year of the present century that gentleman followed the system then just introduced by Mr. Flower, in the *Cambridge Journal*, of "leaders," or "leading articles."

The Leeds newspaper-press boasts of many notable men among its editors — men who gained fame and honour in other walks of literature. Mr. Baines achieved a great reputation by his "History of the County Palatine and Duchy of Lancaster," in four quarto volumes; and his townsmen rendered him only the acknowledgment he had well earned when, in 1834, they elected him as their Parliamentary representative, without canvass or expense to himself. Another author, who first wrote under the pseudonym of "Derwent Conway," namely, Henry D. Inglis, a novelist and writer of many volumes of travel, was for some time editor of the *Leeds Independent*. A third literary man, who founded more newspapers than King Stephen built castles, became editor of the *Leeds Intelligencer* in 1822. This was Alaric Attila Watts, the young poet, who was not to be crushed by the London monthly magazine which found amusement in stupidly calling him "Alaric Choleric Potts

Edward Baines.

Watts!" Mr. Watts did not found, but he may be said to have established, on very effective foundations, the Conservative *Leeds Intelligencer*. The *Leeds Times* had an editor, during the best portion of his career, in that promising young Scottish poet, Robert Nicoll, whose " Bonnie Rowan Bush," and " Bonnie Bessie Lee had a face fu' o' smiles," are only two of many songs that will be heard in the north and read in the south as long as there remain singers in the one and readers in the other. But the delicate young poet found Leeds quite a different sort of place to his native Auchtergaven, to Perth, or to Dundee, in which last town, like Allan Ramsay in Edinburgh, he had kept a circulating library and written lyrics full of sweetness and refinement. Nicoll, an advanced ultra-Radical in politics, as weak in body as he was strong in purpose and fearless in expression, was so badly off in Dundee as to be tempted to settle in Leeds, and accept the editorship of the *Leeds Times* for—*one hundred pounds* a year! His Radical ardour sustained him for a while, but in the fierce local and general political warfare of Leeds, Nicoll's strength, or weakness, could not carry him far. His will survived his power, and he continued the fight as Edmund Kean did in Richard, after he had got his death-stroke, making passes with his swordless arm, and dying as he made them. Robert Nicoll was but 24 when he died, in 1837. More than a generation has since gone by, but the Radical lyrist is still affectionately remembered, not only in Leeds, but wherever in the neighbourhood he carried with him his gentle earnestness and his undying love of song.

QUAKERS' BURIAL GROUND

THE road leading from Oulton to Rothwell follows the boundary line of Oulton Park, and about 200 yards down the road there is an enclosed plot of ground within the park boundary, known as the "Quakers' Garth." This plot of ground was bought by the Quakers in 1721 for a burial-ground, and was used as such for many years, the last burial having taken place in 1820. It has long been enclosed in the park, but is, of course, a separate property. Its distinctive character as a burial place is hidden from the casual passer-by. A look over the park wall, however, shows a square plot of ground, bounded by a stone wall, and thickly overrun with vegetation of a wild, random growth, without stone or marble of any sort to show what it has been. It is most suggestive of a burial place for those (if any such could be) who lived and died without a friend. Not far from the place, and also within the park, is the pretty village church of Oulton, with its graveyard so pleasantly situated, well arranged, and carefully tended. The contrast between the two places is striking, and calculated to raise diverse emotions in a reflective mind.

A RELIC OF ANTIQUITY

An object of great interest and curiosity was ploughed up in 1844 in a field at Scalby, near Scarborough, belonging to the late Mr. Hardcastle, of Scalby Villa. It was a torgue, or collar, of pure gold, wrought in imitation of a cord, and weighing two-and-a-half ounces. It was a badge of dignity, worn round the neck by the ancient Gauls and Britons of high rank. Livy narrates a single combat which took place 358 years before the Christian era between a youthful Roman, Titus Maulius, and a gigantic Gaul, who, like a second Goliah, had come forth between the two armies, and challenged a Roman champion to fight. Maulius slew his opponent, and taking from him a golden torgue, threw it around his own neck, and returning in triumph, was hailed by his fellow-soldiers as Torquatus—henceforward the surname of a leading family of ancient Rome. The golden torgue, or collar, is unique in this part of England, but common elsewhere. It was found by a farmer named Manson, of Scalby, and passed into the possession of Mr. Hardcastle, of that place. Its diameter is eleven inches. Publius Cornelius took 4,070 golden torgues after the slaughter of the Boii (in Gaul). "The British heroine Boadicea wore a golden one of unusual size; and Virdomarus had one fastened behind with hooks, which fell off when he was decapitated. Jornades mentions them as substitutes for diadems. Among the Anglo-Saxons and Normans they were insignia of Dukes and Earls" (*Arch. Dic.*) "An oval amulet, enchased in gold, hung from the Druid's neck." Another account says—"The Druids wore a kind of ornament enchased with gold around their necks, called the Druid's egg," or, by a third account, "the anguinum, or serpent egg of the Druids which was a charm of wonderful power," &c. It is worthy of remark that the torgue, or collar in question, was found on an ancient battle-field.

DUCKING AND CUCKING STOOLS

A mistake commonly made with regard to these instruments of punishment of the olden time is, that they were identical. They were distinct instruments, and were used originally for the punishment of different offences. The ducking-stool was employed *chiefly* as a correction for scolding women; but with doubtful success, I fancy. With respect to the cucking-stool, the following extract from Chambers's "Book of Days," Vol. 1. p. 211, will explain what it was:—

"The term *Cucking-stool* is sometimes used interchangeably for ducking-stool, the resemblance of the names having apparently led to an idea that they meant the same thing. In reality the cucking-stool was a seat of a kind which delicacy forbids us particularly to describe, used for the exposure of flagitious females at their own doors or in some other public place, as a means of putting upon them the last degree of ignominy. In Scotland an ale-wife who exhibited bad drink to the public was put upon the *Cock Stule*, and the ale, like such relics of John Girder's feast as were totally uneatable (see *Bride of Lammermoor*), was given to the pure folk. In Leicester, in 1457, a scold was put upon the cuck-stool before her own door, and then carried to the four gates of the town. The practice seems a strange example of the taste of our ancestors; yet, in connection with the fact, it is worthy of being kept in mind that among the ceremonies formerly attending the installation of the Pope was the public placing of him in a similar chair, called the *Sedes Stercoraria*, with a view to remind him that he was after all but a mortal man."

We gather from this extract that on one occasion at least a scold was subjected to the punishment of the *cuck-stool*. We of the present day should be greatly shocked and scandalised if the power of inflicting such an infamous punishment on women as that of the ducking-stool were by law placed in the hands of an Archbishop. But that such was actually the case at one period of our history, witness the following:—
"At this time" (about A.D. 1120) "the Archbishop" (Thurstan of York) "exercised almost regal authority in his baronies of Beverley, Ripon, Scireburn, Patrington, Otley, and Wilton. He had prisons and Justices in these towns, with full power to try, condemn, and execute criminals. He had returns of writs, pleas of withernam, the taking of estreats by the hands of the Sheriffs for levying the King's debts upon those persons who had nothing without his liberties. He had a gallows, pillory, and *cucking-stool* in all the above-named towns."—*Oliver's* "*Beverley*," pp. 85, 86.

During the episcopate of John le Romaine—1286 to 1296—we find the people bestirring themselves with the view of curtailing the civil power of the ecclesiastic, *e.g.*, "Amongst the pleas of *quo warranto*, a writ was issued against John le Romaine, Archbishop of York, to examine by what authority he claimed to have, within the boroughs of Beverley and Ripon, infangthef and utfangthef, markets and fairs, personal property, (*catalla*) a gallows and a gibbet, a pillory and a *cucking stool*, judgment of fugitives and felons, wreck and waif, fines for the escape of thieves, coroners for prizes, return of writs, custody of prisoners and gaol delivery, pleas *de frisca forcia et vetito namia*, and other pleas which ought to belong to the sheriff; why neither sheriff nor bailiff of the King was suffered to enter into his two boroughs of Beverley and Ripon to exercise the duties of his office; why the King's Justices were not permitted to hold pleas or try prisoners within the liberties of these boroughs; on what authority he claims to have a park in Beverley; and to ascertain whether, for these privileges, he has the lawful authority of the King, or any of his predecessors." To which the Archbishop answered, that he claimed all these *privileges* by *virtue of his office*, from charter, and ancient usage; and proceeded to give a copious enumeration of all his rights and immunities within the boroughs of Beverley and Ripon. To give a complete list of all his claims would take up far too much space, but among the number, " he claimed, *ab antiquo*, in Beverley and Ripon, to have a gallows and a gibbet, with the *privilege* of executing criminals without appeal to the King. He further laid claim to the right of having at Beverley and Ripon a pillory and *cucking stool* (pilliorium et tumbellum), and fines ou the escape of felons." Pp. 109, 110, 111. Most of the italics in this extract are mine. Strange claims, surely, for one who, holding such a position, ought to have been imbued with the spirit of his Lord and Master, and whose motto ought to have been, " Blessed are the merciful, for they shall obtain mercy." At p. 428 Oliver further says, "This machine, called otherwise the trebucket or trap-door, was of very great antiquity in Beverley. It was placed in Bar-dyke, and exhibited *in terrorem*, to keep that unruly member, the female tongue, in due subjection. Many instances occur, however, of hardy females who have undauntedly braved the punishment rather than surrender the invaluable privilege which a woman holds most dear. About the middle of the last century this machine was finally removed and the punishment abolished; but the place where it stood is still distinguished by the name of Ducking-stool Lane." It is hardly necessary to point out that in the above extracts, *mutato nomine*, the "ducking-stool" is meant.

In the *London Evening Post* of 27th April, 1745, we read—" Last week a woman that keeps the Queen's Hotel alehouse at Kingston, in Surrey, was ordered by the Court to be ducked for scolding, and was accordingly placed in the chair and ducked in the river Thames, under Kingston Bridge, in the presence of 2,000 or 3,000 people."

In 1824 a woman was, at Philadelphia, in America, sentenced " to be placed in a certain instrument of correction called a *cucking* or ducking stool, and plunged three times into the water;" but the Supreme Court of Pennsylvania rescinded this order, and decided that " the punishment was obsolete and contrary to the spirit of the age." (N. and Q., 1st series, vol IX., p. 232). Here again it will be noticed that the two instruments are evidently considered identical.

There is an old ducking-stool in the Museum at Scarborough, where anyone interested in local antiquities, and who may visit this watering-place, may gratify his curiosity by a sight of it.

Bolton Percy.   F. W. JACKSON, M.A.

WIFE SALES IN YORKSHIRE

Amongst the popular errors which have existed in the minds of the most ignorant of the population may be classed the strange belief that the marriage tie could be dissolved by the sale of the wife by public auction, and a good deal of surprise was felt in many villages by the ignorant peasantry at the result of a trial at the West Riding Sessions, June 28th, 1837, where a man named Joshua Jackson was convicted of selling his wife, and sentenced to imprisonment for one month with hard labour.—On the 4th of February, 1806, a man named George Gowthorp, of Patrington, sold his wife in the Market-place of Hull for the sum of twenty guineas, and with a halter delivered her to a person named Houseman.—In 1815 a man held a regular auction in the Market-place at Pontefract, offering his wife at the minimum bidding of one shilling, and " knocked her down " for eleven shillings.—In 1858, in a beershop in Little Horton, Bradford, a man named Hartley Thompson put up his wife, described by the local journals at the time as a "pretty young woman," for sale ; he even announced the sale beforehand by means of a crier or bellman, and brought her in with a ribbon round her neck, by way of halter. These two persons had lived unhappily together, and both entertained a belief that by such a process as this they could legally separate for life. At Selby, in the month of December, 1862, a man publicly sold his wife on the steps of the Market-cross for a pint of ale.

Pudsey.   S. Rayner.

RIDING THE STANG

Norrisson Scatcherd, F.S.A., gives the following description of this ancient custom : " Riding the Stang, upon a fight between husband and wife, was in common use in Morley during the last century, but is now discontinued. A wanton wag, upon these occasions, was carried on a stang or pole, he was followed by a number of such mischievous dogs as himself, and was set down or mounted on a wall when the ᐧNomine' was to be repeated." Another custom was called, " pack sheeting." " When two persons have been united in wedlock, if either party has had other sweethearts, the unsuccessful are taken by their companions and tossed into a wool pack sheet, with a few hearty knocks on the ground, purposely inflicted, until the patient consents to pay a small fine to be spent for the general good. This imposition is termed paying socket." This custom of levying " socket " was also practised upon any person who came " a-courting" from any of the neighbouring villages to Morley. Another obsolete custom is that of " Trashing " or pelting common people with old shoes, on their return from church, upon the wedding day.

OLD THREE LAPS

William Sharp, *alias* "Old Three Laps," lived and died at Whorls, or as it is sometimes called World's End, a lonely farm-house nearly two miles to the north-west of Keighley, and about half a mile north of the village of Laycock. He was the son of a respectable farmer, and from a youth was eccentric in his habits. At the age of thirty he went to Keighley Church to be married to a young woman to whom he had formed an attachment, but whose parents, disapproving of the union, kept her at home. Sharp at once returned home and went to bed, in a small room nine feet square, vowing that he never more would leave it, and he kept his resolution. The room had a stone floor, a fireplace, and a smoky chimney, on account of which a fire could seldom be tolerated. The window was fastened down, and the lower panes boarded to prevent inquisitive people from looking in. "The furniture comprised an old oak clock, minus weights and pendulum, almost covered with a thick network of cobwebs, a small round table of dark oak, and a plain, unvarnished, four-post bedstead without hangings." In this bed and unventilated room he remained for 38 years, obstinately refusing to speak even to his constant attendant, and forbidding any one else to enter his room. If visitors intruded, he covered himself with the bedclothes, and on one occasion tore a hole in the tick and buried himself in the feathers. His father by will provided for his sustenance, and for an attendant. He did ample justice to the food procured for him, and became excessively stout. His flesh was thick and firm, and his estimated weight was about 240 pounds. "He ate his meals in a curious way, for his legs became contracted, and drawn up towards his body, and when about to eat his food he used to roll himself over, and so take his meals in a kneeling posture, and to prevent any crumbs getting into the blankets on which he lay, he turned the under blanket over, and ate them off the bed tick." He died on Monday, March 3rd, 1856, saying, " Poor Bill, poor Bill, poor Bill Sharp." He had not uttered so connected a sentence for many years. "Thousands assembled in Keighley Church and graveyard, where he was buried, to pay their last tribute of wonder at his obsequies. The coffin excited much attention from its extraordinary size, being more like a great oak chest than a coffin; it was two feet four inches in depth, and so heavy that it required eight men with strong ropes to lower it into the grave. The weight of the coffin and its contents was estimated at 480 lbs. It was put together in the room in which he died, and the window and part of the wall had to be removed to get it out."

Leeds.   C. D. H.

THE CUSTOM OF HORN-BLOWING

THERE is no doubt about the custom of "blowing of a horn in winter," within the last hundred years, although we have as yet found no record of such a thing being done. Horn-blowing having originated in Saxon times, the crafty Normans after the conquest turned the circumstance to their own account. Land tenures were granted on condition of their having all the horn-blowing to themselves, and the poor crushed inhabitants were glad to do any amount of cringing for rewards. In the *Britannia*, drawn up by the antiquary Gough, is the following, and I beg the reader to notice the words I have italicized :—

"Bradford belonged to John of Gaunt, who granted to John Northrop, of Manningham, and his heirs, three messuages and six bovates of land, *to come to Bradford on the blowing of a horn in winter* and to wait upon him and his heirs on their way from Blackburnshire, with a lance and hunting dog, for thirty days; to have for yeoman's board, one penny for himself, and a half-penny for his dog. A descendant of this Northrop afterwards granted land to Rushworth, of Horton, to hold the lance while Northrop's man blew the horn. The name of Hornman, or Hornblowing Land, was imposed upon the lands in question, and the custom is still kept up. A man comes into the market place with a halbert, a horn, and a dog, and is there met by the owner of the lands in Horton. After the proclamation made, the former calls aloud,—Heirs of Rushworth, come hold me my hound, while I blow three blasts of my horn, to pay the rent due to our Sovereign Lord the King. He then delivered the String to the man from Horton, and winds his horn thrice. The Original horn resembles that at Tutbury in Staffordshire, and is still preserved, though stripped of its original ornaments." So far Gough, who may have seen the *real* horn, though it is now a matter of doubt whether the one formerly in the possession of the Bradford Philosophical Society is the real or a fictitious one. Both the custom and the horn are no doubt coeval with the origin of the Bradford arms, which contain three bugle horns. The day in winter when the horn was first blown was St. Martin's day, November 11th, when the sun sets at a little after four o'clock, and the temperature of the air has reached about 43 degrees.

The custom of blowing a horn at five o'clock in summer, and at six in winter, at Wyke, to rouse the people to their daily labour, was only discontinued quite recently. This shows how a custom may be kept up although done for another purpose. The horn was blown at Bainbridge for the guidance of travellers; at Bradford, to pay the rent of the land; and at Wyke to wake the people in the morning. The late Rev. W. Houlbrook, of Wyke, had the horn formerly used in his possession until his death. This gentleman was Vicar of Wyke for almost thirty years. He was a kind genial gentleman and an industrious antiquary.

Eldwick, near Bingley.　　　　　　　　　　ABRAHAM HOLROYD.

ANCIENT CROSSES AT ILKLEY

In Whitaker's "History of Craven," we have the following account of these interesting remains of a bygone age :—

In different parts of the churchyard are the remains of three very ancient Saxon crosses, wrought in frets, scrolls, knots, &c., which Camden, with that propensity to error, from which the greatest men are not exempt, conjectured to to be Roman, only because they were placed within the precincts of a Roman fortress. But they are of the same kind, and probably of the same age, with the three crosses of Paulinus at Whalley, and with three others remaining in Leland's time at Ripon, which there is great reason to ascribe to Wilfrid. "One thing," saith that venerable antiquary, "I much noted, that was three crossis standing in rowe at the est ende of the chapel garthe. They were things *antiquissimi operis* and monuments of some notable men buried there; so that of the old monasterie of Ripon (the work of Wilfrid) and the town I saw no likely tokens after the depopulation of the Danes in the place, but only the waulles of our ladie chapelle and the crossis." Such is Leland's conjecture as to the occasion of their being erected ; but, from the same number, three in every instance, it is reasonable to suppose that they were early objects of religious reverence, alluding to the mystery of the Holy Trinity.

The three crosses are now placed on the south side of the churchyard, as they are shewn in the engraving ; and have been carefully examined and described by the late Mr. Wardell. That in the centre is the most entire, and is about eight feet in height; the others have been seriously mutilated by having been at one time made use of as gate posts, but are now, it is hoped, placed beyond the reach of further injury. These venerable relics are sepulchral monuments of the Saxon period, and of the same description as those of which only a few fragments remain at Leeds, Dewsbury, and other places. They are elaborately carved with scroll work and with figures of men, birds, and animals. The *centre one*, which is 16 inches by 14 inches at the base, tapering to 11 inches square at the top, bears on the north side the symbols of the

Evangelists, in oblong compartments, human figures in flowing robes, each with the head of the animal which is his symbol, surrounded by a glory, and holding the book of his gospel. St. John, the uppermost, has the head of an eagle; St. Luke, the next, that of a bull; St. Mark,

Ancient Crosses, Ilkley.

that of a lion; and St. Matthew, a human figure. The south side contains the figure of our Lord, and there appears to have been an inscription above his head, then a device composed of two animals whose lower extremities are knotted together; and then two other monstrous figures. The remaining sides have scroll-work, with representations of fruit and leaves.

The *eastern one* is about five feet in height and one foot square at the base, tapering to nine inches at the top, very much defaced and worn—having been used as a gate post; it bears two men facing each other, then two animals, with their lower extremities interlaced, then two others, and lastly two birds. The remaining two sides—for the fourth is mutilated—are composed of scroll-work.

The *western one* is about four feet in height, and much more worn and defaced than the others; it has on one side a scroll and the figure of an ecclesiastic in robes, holding a book; the designs on the other sides are almost obliterated. In this stone the mortice hole for fixing the cross is yet to be seen.

In the year 1868 a fragment of another cross of this period (see woodcut) was found on removing the foundations of some old cottages, nearly opposite to the church; it has on the upper portion of one side a human figure, with hands raised in the act of prayer. The other sides bear the usual scroll work ornamentation.

A. W. MORANT, F.S.A.

Leeds.

TWO QUAINT CHURCH OFFICES

Dog whippers and sluggard wakers were offices held in connection with the Church in the days of our fathers. The duties of these positions were often performed by one person. In the days of yore many persons felt it their duty to bequeath part of their worldly wealth for the purpose of keeping the congregation awake, and driving stray dogs out of the church. W. Andrews, in an article in the Pantiles Papers for September, 1878, gives many instances of parish accounts, a few of which he furnishes as examples. The Wakefield churchwardens accounts present the following items:—

	£	s.	d.
1616—Paid to Gorly Stork for whippinge doggs	0	2	6
1624—Paid to the dog whipper	0	2	0
1625 / 1628 Paid to Lyght Owler for whippinge doggs	0	1	4

Mr. W. S. Banks says "Dog whipper is the title by which the verger was called for a century or more. The name has come down to our time in the form of 'dog nawper:' 'Nawpin' is striking on the head."

	£	s.	d.
1654—Dogg whipper for his qr. wages	0	4	0
1703—For hatts, shoes, and hoses for sexton and dog whipper	0	18	6

These officials were clothed down to 1820, and there are entries on this account throughout. Barnsley churchwardens' accounts record—

1647—To Richard Hodgson's wife for whipping doggs ..£0 02 00

At East Witton, Yorkshire, was an official known as the dog whipper, who received a salary of 8s. a year.

In the churchwardens' accounts of Barton-on-Humber is an entry—

1740—Paid Brocklebank for waking sleepers 0 2 0

Some of the wands for waking sleepers were fitted up with a kind of a fork at one end, and just fitted the nape of the neck, which the sleep wakener having dexterously adjusted to his victim's neck, shook him up. We have read of a beadle in another church going round the edifice during divine service carrying a long staff, at one end of which was a fox's brush and at the other end a knob. With the former he gently tickled the faces of the female sleepers, while on the heads of their male compeers he bestowed with the knob a sensible rap. In Baslow Church, an ancient chapel of Bakewell, Derbyshire, there is still preserved the implement of a dog whipper. The thong of the whip is about three feet long, and is fastened to a long ash stick, round the handle of which is a band of twisted leather.

Woodhouse.   F. BLACKETT.

BLIND JACK OF KNARESBOROUGH

JOHN METCALFE,* commonly called "Blind Jack," died at Spofforth, about four miles from Knaresborough, April 26th, 1810, in the ninety-third year of his age. His descendants at that time were four children, twenty grandchildren, and ninety great and great great grandchildren. He is, perhaps, one of the most remarkable instances on record, of the difficulties of blindness and want of education being overcome by perseverance and industry. During his long life he was engaged in the most active and diverse employments. He was born at Knaresborough, August 15th, 1717; at the age of six years, he was completely deprived of sight by the smallpox; six months after his recovery, he was able to go from his father's house to the end of the street, and return without a guide. When about nine years of age, he began to associate with other boys, rambling about with them to seek bird nests, and used to climb the trees for his share of the spoils. At the age of thirteen he was taught music, and soon became an able performer; he also learned to ride and swim, and was passionately fond of

---

* The popular derivation of the name of Metcalfe is amusing. On a time when the country abounded with wild animals, two men being in the woods together, at evenfall, seeing a red fourfooted beast coming towards them, could not imagine in the dusk what it was. One said, "Have you heard of lions being in these woods?" The other answered he had, but had never seen any such thing. So they conjectured that what they saw was one. The creature advanced a few paces towards them. One ran away, the other determined to meet it. The animal happened to be a *red calfe*,—so he who met it got the name of *Metcalfe*, and he who ran away, that of *Lightfoot*.

field sports. He began to practice, as a musician, at Harrogate, when twenty-five years of age, and not unfrequently was a guide during the darkness of night over the moors and wilds, then abundant in the neighbourhood of Knaresborough. He was also addicted to horse racing, on which occasions he often rode his own horses. He so tutored his horses, that whenever he called them by their respective names, they would answer by neighing, and he could readily find his own, among any number, without any difficulty or assistance. When he attained the age of manhood, his mind was possessed of a self-dependence, rarely enjoyed by those who have the perfect use of all their faculties, his body was well proportioned to his mind, for, when twenty-one years of age, he was six feet one and a half inches in height, strong, and robust in proportion. Once, being desirous of obtaining some fish, he, unaided, drew a net in the deepest part of the river Wharfe, for three hours together; at one time he held the lines in his mouth, being obliged to swim.

The marriage of this extraordinary individual was a romance in real life, something like that which Sir Walter Scott has described in his ballad of "Lochinvar." Miss Benson, between whom, and our hero, a reciprocal affection had for some time subsisted, was to be married next day, to one Mr. Dickinson, a husband of her parent's choice. The damsel not relishing the match, determined to elope with Metcalfe, blind and poor as he was. They were accordingly married next day, much to the chagrin and disappointment of her parents and their intended son-in-law, and the surprise of all who knew and heard of it, for she was as handsome a woman as any in the country. When afterwards questioned, by a lady, concerning this extraordinary step, and why she had refused so many good offers for "Blind Jack," she answered, "Because I could not be happy without him." And being more particularly questioned, she replied—"His actions are so singular, and his spirit so manly and enterprising, that I could not help liking him."

He continued to play at Harrogate in the season; and set up a four wheel chaise, and a one horse chair, for public accommodation, there having been nothing of the kind there before. He kept these vehicles two summers, when the innkeepers beginning to run chaises, he gave them up, as he also did racing and hunting; but still, wanting employment, he bought horses and went to the coast for fish, which he took to Leeds and Manchester; and so indefatigable was he, that he would frequently walk for two nights and a day, with little or no rest; for, as a family was coming on, he was as eager for business as he had been for diversion, still keeping up his spirits, as Providence blessed him with good health.

More extraordinary still, when the rebellion of 1745 broke out in Scotland, "Blind Jack" joined a regiment of volunteers, raised by Colonel Thomas Thornton, a patriotic gentleman, for the defence of the house of Hanover, shared with them all the dangers of the campaign, defeated at Falkirk, victorious at Culloden. Jack afterwards carried on a small contraband trade, between the ports on the east coast and the interior; as well as in galloways from Scotland, in which he met with many adventures. In the year 1754, he set up a stage waggon between York and Knaresborough, being the first on that road, and conducted it constantly himself twice a-week in the summer season, and once in the winter, which occupation he continued until he began to contract for making roads, which suited him better. The first contract of the kind which he had, was three miles between Minskip and Ferransley, on the Boroughbridge and Knaresborough road.[*] He afterwards made hundreds of miles of road in Yorkshire, Lancashire, Cheshire, and Derbyshire; he also built bridges and houses. He was a dealer in timber and hay, which he used to measure, and then calculate the solid contents, by a peculiar method of his own. The hay he always measured with his arms, and, having learnt the height, he could soon tell the number of square yards in any stack. Whenever he went out, he always carried with him a stout staff, some inches taller than himself, which was of great use to him, both in his travels and measurements. He is thus mentioned in a paper published in the "Memoirs of the Literary and Philosophical Society of Manchester," vol. 1. "His present occupation is that of a projector and surveyor of highways, in difficult and mountainous parts. With the assistance only of a long staff, I have several times met this man traversing the roads, ascending precipices, exploring valleys, and investigating their several extents, forms, and situations, so as to answer his designs in the best manner. The plans which he designs, and the estimates he makes, are done in a method peculiar to himself, and which he cannot well convey the meaning of to others. His abilities, in this respect, are nevertheless so great, that he finds constant employment. Most of the roads over the Peak in Derbyshire have been altered by his directions, particularly those in the vicinity of Buxton; and he is, at this time, constructing a new one between Wilmslow and Congleton, with a view to open a communication with the great London road, without being obliged to pass over the mountains."

In Vol. I. of Dr. Smiles's "Lives of the Engineers," there is a full account of the difficulties Blind Jack encountered while making the road from Huddersfield to Manchester. This was the road along which the clothiers travelled to and from Saddleworth through Marsden to Huddersfield, and on which William Horsfall, of Marsden, was shot by the Luddites. It is the old road past Black Moorfoot, Hollhead, down by Heyheads, through the village of Marsden, up Puleside, and over Standedge; and Dr. Smiles graphically describes the difficulties

---

[*] Dr. Hunter, in his treatise on the Harrogate Waters, has a little bit of dull wit on Blind Jack's road making—"They employed a blind man to lay out the roads in the neighbourhood, upon the ingenious principle, probably, that where such an individual could travel, another with two eyes might surely follow."

Blind Jack encountered in making a good road through the Standedge mountain bogs. Since the making of this road, two other highways, with easier gradients, have been made over the Standedge Hills.

Blind Jack, while making the road in the Marsden region, resided at Heyheads, in Marsden, in the centre house of three of modest proportions, which remain to this day, the house Metcalf occupied now

John Metcalf, aged 79.

being tenanted by Enoch Taylor. Blind Jack at that period might be frequently met with at the "Two Dutchmen" and "Old Ram," Juno, still in existence under the same names, in the heart of the village, where his ready wit and the jocularity of his conversation made him a welcome guest. He was fertile in expedients for overcoming what in railway phraseology would be called "engineering difficulties," as the account in Smiles's biography testifies.

Though "a thick drop serene" had quenched his sight, his active mind devised means for the proof of facts that some persons blessed with sight would have failed to discover. He was an excellent judge of horseflesh, and he could readily distinguish a blind horse from one that could see. His method of doing so was as follows :—He coaxed the animal until he appeared to have made acquaintance with it. Then placing one hand on the region of the heart, he passed the other hand smartly before its eyes without touching them. If it could see, the sudden heart-throb told Jack the fact; but if it remained unmoved, he concluded, and correctly, that like himself, the horse was deprived of sight.

During the making of the Standedge road, Jack had not the workmen's wages ready at the exact time, and the latter accordingly summoned him before the Huddersfield magistrates for payment. The magistrates told him that "he ought to have provided against a rainy day." Jack promptly rejoined that "he had provided for *one* rainy day, but that, unfortunately for him, *two* or more rainy days had come together."

After leaving Lancashire in 1792, he settled at Spofforth, and lived with his daughter, on a small farm there, till his death.

Harrogate.   WM GRAINGE.

JOHN JACKSON OF WOODCHURCH

This eccentric individual was born at Woodchurch, near Morley, and the following amusing account of him is given by Norrisson Scatcherd :—"His name was John Jackson, better known as 'Old Trash,' which was his nickname. He lived at a house near on the site of the present inn, at Woodchurch, and taught a school at Lee-Fair. He was a good mechanic, a stone-cutter, land measurer, and I know not what besides; but very slovenly in his person, and had a head through the hair of which, it was thought, a comb did not as often pass as once a year. Jackson wrote a poem upon Harrogate, commencing—

"O Harrogate, O Harrogate, how great is thy fame!
In summer thou art proud, but in winter thou art tame,"

but his mechanical abilities were his chief excellency. He constructed a clock, and in order to make it useful to the clothiers, who attended Leeds Market from Earls and Hanging Heaton, Dewsbury, Chickenley, &c., he kept a lamp suspended near the face of it, and burning through the winter nights, and he would have no shutters or curtains to his window, so that the clothiers had only to stop and look through it to know the time. Now, in this our age of luxury and refinement, the accommodation thus presented by "Old Trash" may seem insignificant and foolish, but I can assure the reader that it was not. The clothiers of the early part of last century were obliged to be upon the bridge of Leeds, where the market was held, by about six o'clock in summer, and seven in winter ; and hither they were convened by a bell anciently pertaining to a chantry chapel, which once was annexed to Leeds Bridge. They did not all ride, but most of them went on foot. They did not all carry watches, but very few of them had ever possessed such a valuable. They did not dine on fish, flesh and fowl, with wine, as some do now. No! no! the careful housewife wrapped up a bit of oatcake and cheese in the little chequed handkerchief, and charged her husband to mind and not get above a pint of ale at "the Rodney." Would Jackson's clock then be of no use to them who had few such in their villages? who seldom saw a watch; but took much of their intelligence from the note of the cuckoo? Jackson was buried, according to the Woodkirk Register, on the 19th of May, 1764."*

In the *Reliquary*, July 1874, we find an account of a journey made by Jackson, in 1755, and the journal which he kept is of the most amusing character, and will, we feel sure, be acceptable to the readers of "Old Yorkshire." The article was contributed to the *Reliquary* by the Rev. Gerard Smith, who says that little is known of the history of the journal. "It belonged to the Rev. William Mason, Rector of Aston, Yorkshire, the friend and biographer of the poet William Gray, and himself a person of refined tastes, and a poet; and it came, together with other literary treasures, into the possession of Mr. Mason's intimate friend and executor, the Rev. Christopher Alderson, who at Mr. Mason's death in 1800, was presented to the Rectory of Aston by the Duke of Leeds. Mr. Alderson died in 1814; his son, and successor in the living, the Rev. Wm. Alderson, becoming heir to his father's literary property, and to this Journal as a part of it. In 1821, he was presented to the Vicarage of Tissington, by his friend Sir H. Fitzherbert, Bart., and died in 1852 in his 80th year; but his widow survives him, and to her kindness we are indebted for this publication of a remarkable MS."

The author, John Jackson, an uneducated but enlightened and judicious observer of men and things, has recorded in its pages the events of a pilgrimage, in the autumn of 1755, from Woodkirk, in the West Riding, to Glastonbury, in Somerset, full of the adventures and hardships of travelling on foot in those days, and of information upon the social state of the country through which he passed. His visit to Gloucester is associated with "Mr. Raikes the printer, my old friend," and afterwards the founder, in 1780, of English Sunday Schools.

Glastonbury Thorn, the main object of John Jackson's journey, continues to bloom at Christmas time, and even earlier—this variety of whitethorn being remarkable for producing blossoms both in the autumn and in the spring—the latter bloom yielding the fruit, which may be seen upon the same branch with the autumn flowers. Similar instances of the concurrence of blossoms and fruit, upon the same tree, are not rare, especially in the pear and apple, and in roses. The original Thorn at Glastonbury is reported, by a Romish legend, to have sprung out of the staff of Joseph of Arimathea—a mode of producing thorns not unknown to gardeners.

---

* Scatcherd's *History of Morley*, p. 220.

JAMES NAYLOR, MAD QUAKER

James Nayler (or Naylor) was born in 1616 at East Ardsley, near Wakefield, where he lived twenty-two years and upwards, until he married, *according to the world,*" as he expressed himself. He dwelt afterwards in the parish of Wakefield, till some time in the Civil War, when he served his country under various officers on the side of the Parliament, and rose to be Quarter-Master under General Lambert. In this service he continued till disabled by illness in Scotland, when he returned home. About this time he was member of an Independent Church at Horbury, of which Christopher Marshall was pastor. By this society being cast out, on charges of blasphemy and incontinence with a Mrs. Roper (a married woman) he turned Quaker. Travelling soon after to visit his quaking brethren in Cornwall, he was arrested by one Major Saunders, and committed as a vagrant; but being released by an order from the Council of State, he bent his course through Chewstoke, in Somersetshire, to Bristol, and here those extraordinary scenes were contemplated which I have to relate.

By way of preliminary, however, I ought to observe that notwithstanding the irregularities in Nayler's life, there were many things in the man which, with low and ignorant people, exceedingly favoured his pretensions to the Messiahship. He appeared, both as to form and to feature, the perfect likeness of Jesus Christ, according to the best descriptions.* His face was of the oval shape, his forehead broad, his hair auburn and long, and parted on the brow, his beard flowing, his

---

* The accompanying portrait is taken from a photograph in the possession of H. Ecroyd Smith, Esq., the latter being taken from the original painting in the possession of the late William Darton, publisher, London.

James Naylor,
The Quaker

eyes beaming with a benignant lustre, his nose of the Grecian or Circassian order, his figure erect and majestic, his aspect sedate, his speech sententious, deliberate, and grave, and his manner authoritative. In addition, also, to these advantages, his studies had been devoted to Scripture history, and by some means he had caught up the Gnostic heresy, and the doctrine of Œons, so that like many of the "experimental" folk (the Gnostics of our day) he could bewilder and confound others without being detected or abashed himself.

The usual posture of Nayler was sitting in a chair, while his company of men and women knelt before him. These, it appears, were very numerous and constant for whole days together. At the commencement of the service a female stepped forth and sung—

"This is the joyful day—
Behold, the king of righteousness is come."

Another taking him by the hand, exclaimed—

"Rise up, my love, my dove, and come away,
Why sittest thou amongst the pots?"

Then, putting his hand upon her mouth, she sank upon the ground before him, the auditory vociferating—

"Holy, holy, holy, to the Almighty!"

The procession of this lunatic and imposter (for lunatic he evidently was) especially in passing through Chepstow, was extensive and singular. Mounted on the back of a horse or mule—one Woodcock preceded him, bareheaded, and on foot—a female on each side of Nayler, held his bridle; many spread garments in his way, while the ladies sung—

"Hosannah to the Son of David! Blessed is he that cometh in the name of the Lord! Hosannah to the highest!"

But this was only a portion of the incense which was offered as homage to this messiah, for the letters of the fair sex addressed to him were of the warmest and most flattering description. They called him "Jesus," "The Prophet of the Most High," "The King of Israel and the Prince of Peace." It needs scarcely to be added, but the fact is, they paid him frequently a tribute equally acceptable to prophets, priests, and kings.

I know not what sort of a prophet James Nayler was, but I am sure he could not be a worse one than Richard Brothers, Johanna Southcott, and all other such pretenders as have since arisen; he wrought, however, according to the allegation of Dorcas Erbury, a capital miracle upon her, for he raised her from the dead in Exeter Gaol, after she had departed this life full two days; and that is more than all the Towsers, Mousers, and Carousers of Johanna, or the prophetess herself ever did, as they would perhaps acknowledge. It is highly probable, however, that the miracles of James Nayler did not end here, since to a messiah so highly gifted as he was, it would be much easier, and more natural, to produce a Shiloh with the concurrence of Dorcas Erbury, than to bring back her departed spirit to the world it left. Be this as it may, the House of Commons, in 1656, was so sceptical, so irreligious, and so insensible to the merits of this Quaker-Christ, that on Wednesday, the 17th of December, in that year, after a patient investigation of ten days, it was resolved—" That James Nayler be set on the pillory with his head in the pillory, in the Palace-yard, Westminster, during the space of two hours, on Thursday following, and should be whipped by the hangman through the streets from Westminster to the Old Exchange, London, and there likewise be set with his head in the pillory for the space of two hours, between the hours of eleven and one on Saturday after, in each place, wearing a paper containing an inscription of his crimes; and that at the Old Exchange his tongue be bored through with a hot iron, and that he be there stigmatized also with the letter 'B' on the forehead; and he be afterwards sent to Bristol, and be conveyed into and through the said city on horseback, bare-ridged, with his face backward, and there also publicly whipped the next Market-day after he comes thither; and that, from thence, he be committed to prison to Bridewell, London, and there restrained from the Society of all people, and there to labour hard till he be released by Parliament, and during that time to be debarred the use of pen, ink, and paper, and have no relief but what he earned by his daily labour." *

"This sentence was for the most part executed upon Nayler, when some of his followers were so infatuated as to lick his wounds, kiss his feet, and lean upon his bosom. He was, however, allowed pen, ink, and paper, and wrote several books during his confinement."

"When lodged in Bridewell, in order to carry on his impostures, he fasted three days, but flesh and blood being able to hold out no longer, he fell to work to earn himself some food."

During the time of Nayler's travels and imprisonment he had frequent recourse to the press. Some of his writings were doctrinal, and many of them controversial.

This narrative is chiefly taken from the State trials, but a curious MS. now before me states that he retracted his errors, was discharged from prison the 8th of September, 1659, and was again received by the Quakers, who had disowned him during his extravagances. It further states that he set out from London the latter end of October, 1660, in order to return to his wife and children at Wakefield, but was

---

* What dreadful sufferings, with what patience he endured, even to the boring through of his tongue with red-hot irons, without a murmur; and with what strength of mind when the delusion he had fallen into, which they stigmatized as blasphemy, had given way to clearer thoughts, he could renounce his error in a strain of the beautifullest humility, yet keep his first grounds and be a Quaker still!—so different from the practice of your common converts from enthusiasm, who, when they apostatize, *apostatize all*, and think they can never get far enough from the society of their former errors, even to the renunciation of some saving truths, with which they had been mingled, not implicated.—*Charles Lamb.* Note by Ed.

taken ill on the road, some miles beyond Huntington, being robbed by the way and left bound, in which condition he was found in a field, by a countryman towards evening, and carried to a friend's house, at Holme near Kings Repton, but soon expired in November, 1660."*

The publications of James Nayler are as follows :—

1. "An Exhortation to the Rulers—the Preachers and Lawyers, 1653."
2. "Milk for Babes and Meat for Strong Men—A Feast of Fat things, Wine well-refined on the Leas, etc.—being the breathings of the Spirit through his Servant James Nayler, written by him during the confinement of his *outward man* in prison, London, 1661."
3. "Nayler's Salutation to the Seed of God, 1656."
4. "An Answer to Blome's Fanatic History."

Morley, near Leeds   *The late* N. SCATCHERD, F.S.A.

OLD MOTHER SHIPTON

YORKSHIRE has produced many notable men and women, but it may be doubted if any of them have ever attained the persistent and world-wide fame of Mother Shipton. For one hundred and forty years edition after edition has been issued from the press of her oracular sayings. He name has become familiar in our mouths as household words, and yet if we ask, in the critical spirit of the modern time, it must be admitted that History is silent respecting her, and that all we have to depend upon is the vague voice of Tradition. The date of her birth is stated by one account to have been 1486 or 1488, whilst another account says that she died in 1651, at the age of seventy! No record of her existence appeared in print until a century and a half after the supposed date of her entrance into this world. The scanty references to her in the works of the historians of Yorkshire are all evidently based upon local traditons or on the pamphlets issued in the seventeenth century. Hargrove and Allen state that she was born in 1488, near the Dropping Well Knaresborough, and that her prophecies had been preserved in MS. in Lord P—'s family.† These pamphlets do not give us any great clue as to the individuality of the prophetess. Much in them is purely imaginative, and only interesting as a specimen of

---

* For other interesting particulars of Nayler's career, see Baring Gould's "*Yorkshire Oddities.*" Ed.

† Probably Lord Powis. In Sloane, MS. 647—4, fol. 89, there is a piece entitled, "A Prophecy found in ye manuscript in ye year 1620." A woman born in 1488 would, however, scarcely be capable of prophesying mundane events in 1620. The MS. contains no name, but the verses have been given as a prediction of Mother Shipton's, coupled with a statement that she died in 1651, when she was over seventy. There is a discrepancy of more than a century in the two dates given for her birth. (See *Oddfellows' Magazine*, July, 1881, p. 168.)

the grotesque in popular literature. As there is proverbially fire where there is smoke, we may, perhaps, assume that some sybil living by the Dropping Well at Knaresborough, acquired a reputation for foreseeing

THE FAMOUS MOTHER SHIPTON

the future, and that her dark sayings were repeated from mouth to mouth until some lucky wight, perhaps a Londoner brought northwards by the royal progresses which preceded the civil war, bethought him of committing them to print. This was in 1641, and in 1645 they were reprinted by the famous William Lilly, who was a firm believer in astrology, and collected a number of ancient and modern prophecies.

Her fame in the seventeenth century was very great. Pepys, in his diary under date 20th October, 1666, writes of Sir Jeremy Smith : "He says he was on board the ' Prince' when the news came of the burning of London ; and all the Prince said was, that now Shipton's prophecy was out,"

But if History is silent Tradition has been very busy with her name. Many predictions are attributed to her. A number of these have recently been gathered by Mr. William Grainge, and printed in the *Palatine Note-book* for April, 1881. From this article we take the following :—

Scarcely any event hereabouts of more than ordinary importance can occur but we are gravely told that "Mother Shipton's prophecy has come to pass" therein or thereby. Should the spring be late, the summer be cold, or snow fall earlier than usual, we are at once told that Mother Shipton prophesied that " we should not know winter from summer, except by the leaves on the trees, before the world was at an end." When railways began to spread throughout the country, Mother Shipton had, in the popular belief, foreseen them, and had said—

" When carriages without horses run,
Old England will be quite undone."

This, like many other equivocal sayings, may be said to be realised in the new state of things which the extension of railways has been the means of introducing into the country ; so that *old England* may be said to be *undone* by the rapid growth of *young England*.

When the railway was being made between Harrogate and York, a lofty viaduct was needed to cross the river Nidd at Knaresborough, which was nearly completed, when through some deficiency in the construction the whole fabric fell into the water ! The popular voice at once declared that Mother Shipton had said that " the big brig across the Nidd should tummle doon twice and stand for ivver when built the third time." The second fall and the third building are yet in the future. This prophecy was never heard by anyone until after the catastrophe occurred.

Prophecies of this kind are not confined to the immediate locality where the prophetess was born ; they are spread over the country far and wide ; and they exist in North-East Lancashire. Our seer predicted that Pickhill, a parish town in the North Riding, would never thrive until a certain family became extinct, and *Picts*, or Money-hill, an old barrow or burial mound adjoining it, should be cut open. Both these events came to pass ; the family indicated became extinct in the year 1850 ; and Money-hill was cut open, and nearly all removed by the formation of the Leeds Northern Railway in 1851. Will the place thrive better now ?

Another of "Shipton's wife's prophecies" had reference to the Castle Hill at Northallerton, a mound which she declared should be filled with blood. The place has become a cemetery for the burial of the dead, which in a limited sense is a fulfilment of the saying ; for we must bear in mind that the utterances of the most gifted seers if tied down to exact literality will often be found wanting.

Another of her predictions was fulfilled at the antique village of Ulleskelfe-on-the-Wharfe. The said village had from time immemorial possessed a large tithe-barn, and a public spring of water called " the Keld." Our prophetess declared that a public road should run through the barn, and the Keld be dried up. No one could believe that such things would happen ; tithe-barns would exist and water spring for ever. Yet the making of the York and North Midland Railway effected both these seeming impossibilities; the iron roadway was laid directly over the place where the barn had stood, and the Keld was removed to another place.

An unfulfilled prophecy relates to Walkingham Hill, a ridge of high land some three miles northward of Knaresborough. The old dame is reported to have said that a time would come when all the hill would run with blood; but with what kind of blood she said not. If the swarms of rabbits which infest it be meant, the prediction is fulfilled every day.

She is also said to have foreseen the use of the Harrogate waters, the building of that town, and the railway bridges leading to it, and to have given her prescience shape and expression in the following very rude lines which have evidently been made in the neighbourhood, for they bear no signs of Cockney manufacture :—

"When lords and ladies stinking water soss,
High brigs o' stean the Nidd sal cross,
An' a toon be built on Harrogate Moss."

The first and last predictions at one time were not likely to come to pass, if they were really uttered before the events; they are, however, now literally fulfilled, for lords and ladies come from all parts of the kingdom to *drink* (synonymous with *soss*) the strong and *stinking* sulphur waters. Harrogate Moss has been reclaimed from the rude Forest of Knaresborough, of which it formed a part, and one of the most elegant towns in the county of York has been built upon it, entirely through the influence of those stinking waters which persons of high breeding are said to *soss*. Two rather lofty viaducts across the river Nidd conduct the railways from the north and east to the town, and these, we suppose, are the "high brigs o' stean" meant by the prophetess. The highest brig is, however, on the south, across the valley of the Cumple, which is not noticed. This prediction is probably not more than thirty years old.

The latest application of the old sybil's name to a recent event took place last year, 1880, when the village of Fewston, which is built partly upon a moving landslip, gave a slight move, cracking the walls of about a dozen houses from the bottom to the top, and appearing as though it would slide down into one of the large reservoirs which the Leeds Corporation has constructed in the valley of the Washburn for the purpose of supplying that town with water. When the slip took place the credulous and alarmed people (or some of them) declared that Mother Shipton had prophesied that Fewston Village should slide into Washburn river before the world was at an end.

Nor are these traditions confined to Yorkshire. In East Norfolk she is made to say :—" The town of Yarmouth shall become a nettlebush. That the bridge shall be pulled up; and small vessels sail to Irstead and Barton Roads." Also, " Blessed are they that live near Potter Heigham, and double-blessed them that live in it.[*]

In Somerset one of Mother Shipton's prophecies was due to come true on Good Friday of 1879, when Ham Hill was to have been swallowed up by an earthquake, and Yeovil swept by a deluge. Large numbers went as near as they thought safe, to see it; many of the inhabitants of the threatened district, more consistently with the state of their belief, fled from their homes and took refuge with friends at some distance. As the stroke of twelve approached, when the awful event was to " come off," there was a queer feeling, mixed of terror and unbelief, prevading the air. When all was over, and the clock was silent, and the disappointed crowd had to disperse, there was a better

---

[*]Harrison : Mother Shipton Investigated, p. 64.

chance for rational faith than there has been in those parts since Mother Shipton's own day.

If asked, "Who was Mother Shipton?" many in reply to such a question would say "A famous prophetess, who foretold the invention of the telegraph, the use of steam, and who declared that the end of the world should be in the year 1881." These prophecies were contained in some well-known lines, devoid of either rhythm or sense. Mr. Charles Hindley has since confessed that he fabricated this doggerel in order to sell an edition of Shipton which he printed in 1862. That Mr. Hindley was not the first to credit Mother Shipton with predictions of which she was quite innocent is evident from an anecdote told by an anonymous correspondent of *Notes and Queries*.[*]

At one of the debates in the Cambridge Union, Praed followed a speaker who had indulged in a vein of gloomy vatication, and Praed said that the speech brought to his mind a prophecy of Mother Shipton, which his facile powers of versification enabled him to manufacture on the spot.[†]

This is by no means a new trick. Throughout the middle ages prophecies were freely employed by the different contending parties in order to strengthen their hold upon the public, and allusions to accomplished events were freely interpolated, in order to give greater credit to prognostications of the future, in which the wish was father to the thought.

The earliest edition of Mother Shipton's prophecy is that printed in 1641. It opens in a very abrupt fashion with a statement that she had predicted that Wolsey should never be at York. Drake, the historian of York, says that the Cardinal never came nearer to the city than Cawood, and after a reference to the prophecy adds, " I should not have noticed this idle story, but that it is fresh in the mouths of our country people at this day; but whether it was a real prediction, or raised after the event, I shall not take upon me to determine. It is more than probable, like all the rest of these kind of tales, the accident gave occasion to the story." After the Wolsey prophecy follow a number of others, some of local and some of general application. Although printed as prose many are in rhyme, and some are certainly of considerable antiquity, having passed current under various other names before they were credited to Mother Shipton. Mr. W. C. Hazlitt mentions another edition published in the same year, which professes to have been taken down in 1625, from the mouth of Jane Waller, who died in March, 1641, at the age of 94, and of whom it is said Mother Shipton had prophesied that she would live to hear of war within the kingdom, but not to see it. The editions since printed have for the most part been uncritical jumbles of various portions of Head's book and the earlier tracts. They are now carefully reprinted, so that

---

[*] 2nd s. xi. 97.   [†] *Notes and Queries*, 2nd s. xi. 33.

all who are interested may see what was the original form of the famous Yorkshire prophecy.

A word may be said in conclusion as to the memorials and portraits of Mother Shipton At one time a sculptured stone, near Clifton, was regarded by the people as a monument to Mother Shipton. In reality it was a mutilated effigy of a knight in armour, which had probably been taken from a tomb in St. Mary's Abbey, and set up as a boundary stone. It is now in the Museum of the Yorkshire Philosophical Society.*

In Rackstow's Museum, Fleet Street, London, there was in 1792, " a figure of Mother Shipton, the prophetess, in which the lineaments of extreme old age are strongly and naturally marked. Also her real skull, brought from her burial place at Knaresborough, in Yorkshire."†

In 1874 Mrs. Banks came across an old painting of the prophetess in the back parlour of a shop in North London. " The somewhat dingy walls were," she says, " to my great surprise, hung with fine old paintings in old frames, and seemed to me of great value. Amongst these my attention was arrested by one larger than the others—an ancient portrait of character so remarkable that I could not refrain from asking whose it might be. The answer was, 'Dame Shipton,' our ancestress, commonly called Mother Shipton, and said by some to be a witch."

An engraving of Mother Shipton, in a chariot drawn by a reindeer or stag, appeared in the *Wonderful Magazine*, Vol. II., London, 1793.

In Kirby's *Wonderful Museum* (Vol. II., p. 145) there is a portrait of Mother Shipton, drawn by Sir Wm. Ouseley, from an oil painting in the possession of Mr. Ralph Ouseley, of York, which had been "present with the family of the proprietor for more than a century." It represents a melancholy-looking woman, with a broad-brimmed hat, whose chin is being stroked by a monkey or familiar.

Mr. Harrison is of opinion that the hooked nose, turned-up chin, and peaked cap of Mother Shipton, as shown in the picture on the edition of the prophecies issued in 1663, became gradually transformed into the figure of *Punch*, with which we are all so familiar. This theory he supports with much ingenuity in his little book, " Mother Shipton Investigated," From a work, entitled " Mother Shipton," published by A. Heywood and Son.

---

* *Notes and Queries*, 4th s., ii., 84.   † *Notes and Queries*, 4th s., iv., 213.

HISTORICAL OAKS, ELMS & YEWS

THE principal object in the township of Headingley, near Leeds, is a venerable oak, which has defied the storms of a thousand winters, and which for hundreds of years has presented to the observers a decaying memorial of ages long since passed away. This remarkable tree has been conjectured by some, and the supposition is warranted by its evidently extreme antiquity, to have witnessed the religious rites of the ancient Britons, and, in fact, to have formed a part of a Druidical grove. Universal tradition declares this to have been the tree under which, in Saxon times, the shire meetings were held, and from which the name of Skyrack (or Shire-oak) has been imposed upon the wapentake. Of course, these traditions afford no positive demonstration, but in spite of scepticism, they render the supposition extremely probable, and induce the conclusion that it must be founded on fact. There are several engravings of this celebrated old "Skyrack Oak," which is alleged (as before said) to have given name to the wapentake of Skyrack (originally Scire-oak); but Whitaker thinks that this supposition is probably a false one. As to the "patriarchal plant" itself, this careful writer says—"Stripped, however, of this adventitious and doubtful fame, it is a venerable object . . and fills the mind with reflections, which individual though unconscious existence, through a period of many centuries, will always excite."

The wapentake of Barkstone Ash is also named from a tree, though of inferior rank and duration to the oak. Undoubtedly these assemblies were anciently held in the open air, and their places were often fixed by some conspicuous natural object. But it must be remembered that though this individual tree may, without any violation of probability, be allowed to have existed in Saxon times, yet, at a period when more than half the country was overspread by forests of indigenous oak, it is, perhaps, too much to assign to the survivor of so many thousands of its own species in an extensive district the honour of having supplied it with a name.

There is another "shire-oak," so named from its peculiar local situation, standing on a spot where the counties of Derby, Nottingham, and York join. It is one of the largest in the kingdom. The area which it covers is 707 square yards.

Of all European trees, the yew is that which attains the greatest age. The three yew trees at the ancient abbey of Fountains, near Ripon, were well known as early as 1132, for the monks are said to have held their services under them before the Abbey was built. Pennant says that in 1770 they were 1,214 lines in diameter, and consequently, according to De Candolle's method of computation, were more than twelve centuries old. Of course there are some others in some parts of the country still older. Many Norman churches in England are to be found with yew trees beside them much older than the churches. Before the founding of Fountains Abbey in 1132 (according to Burton's "Monst. Ebor.") there stood a large elm in the midst of the vale, on which the monks put some thatch or straw; and under that they lay, ate, and prayed, the Bishop for a time supplying them with bread and the rivulet with drink. Part of the day some spent in making wattles to erect a little oratory, whilst others cleared some ground to make a little garden. But it it is supposed that they soon changed the shelter of their elm for that of seven yew trees growing on the declivity of the hill on the south side of the abbey, all yet standing in the year 1810, except the largest, which was blown down about the middle of the last century. They are of an extraordinary size; the trunk of one of them is 26 feet 6 inches in circumference at the height of three feet from the ground. Now they stand so near each other as to form a cover almost equal to a thatched roof. "Under these trees, we are told by tradition, the monks resided till they built the monastery, which seems very probable, if we consider how little a yew tree increases in a year, and to what bulk these are grown. And as the hill-side was covered with wood, which is now almost all cut down except these trees, it seems as if they were left standing to perpetuate the memory of the monks' habitation there during the first winter of their residence."

There is an enormous and very old Wych elm in the gardens of Sir Joseph Copley, at Sprotborough, near Doncaster; and there is also a very ancient tree called "the Abbot's Elm," at Easby Abbey, near Richmond, Yorkshire; to which the following lines have been inscribed:—

> Ancient of days! that midst the dead
> Thy verdant crest still rears,
> Tell us thy wondrous history,
> Sage of a thousand years!

>   Hid in thy forest sanctuary,
>   Unreach'd by light divine,
>   Thou may'st have view'd the unholy rites
>   That stain'd the Druid's shrine.
>
>   . . . .
>
>   Thou, 'midst the wreck, in changeless youth,
>   Still mock'st the wintry blast;
>   Empires are crush'd ;—thou ling'rst on,
>   Historian of the past!
>
>   And though the levelling scythe of Time
>   Past glories may o'erwhelm,
>   Woe to the wretch, whose caitiff hand
>   Shall strike "the Abbot's Elm!"

The "Abbot's Elm" is withered at the top and bereft of many of its branches. Now the roost of owls, ravens, and other birds of reputed ill-omen, it was once a witness of the flourishing state of this abbey; and under its shade many a portly monk may have basked through a summer's day in all the indolence of monastic pride. At a middle distance between the gateway and village, the old walls give an echo very distinct, and which clearly reverberates three or four times.

The old town of Thirsk consists of a long range of cottages on each side of the turnpike road, and of two squares, surrounded by the same kind of buildings. In one of these squares, called St. James's Green, the cattle fairs are held; the other is the site of an ancient church, of which time has long since swept away every vestige. In the latter of these squares is a large elm tree of venerable antiquity, from which the place takes its name, Hawm (*i.e.* Elm) Green; and under the shade of whose branches the Members of Parliament were elected. It was on this spot that Henry Percy, Earl of Northumberland, and lieutenant of the county, is said to have been put to death by the mob, during a popular commotion in the reign of Henry the Seventh. Tradition says that he was dragged from Topcliffe, a village four miles distant from Thirsk, and beheaded at this place, under the shadow of the great elm tree.

At a short distance above the great gateway of Bolton Priory stood the "Prior's Oak," which was felled about the year 1720, and sold for £70. According to the price of wood at that time, it could not contain less than 1,400 feet of timber.

A slip from the Glastonbury Thorn, planted in Birstal Churchyard, near Leeds, about twenty years previously, is stated to have budded on old Christmas Day, in 1782, the weather being remarkably warm for the season. Respecting the original thorn, tradition says that Joseph of Arimathea, preaching at Glastonbury on a Christmas Day, spoke of the birth of Christ, which his hearers being backward in believing, he proposed to strike his staff into the ground as a test of the truth of what he had related, when it is said to have immediately put forth buds and blossoms.

Ribston Park, near Wetherby, is remarkable for being the place where that delicious apple called the "Ribstone Pippin" was first cultivated in this kingdom. The original tree was raised from a pippin brought from France, and from it such numbers have been propagated that they are now to be met with in almost every orchard in this and several other counties. But this multiplication of the trees has not diminished the value of the fruit, which is still preferred before every other apple produced in the English orchards. The old tree is probably yet standing. In the year 1787 it produced six bushels of fruit. There is also a fine collection of pines and firs.

There is a tradition in the neighbourhood of Sandal Castle, Wakefield, that the willow trees just beyond Manygates Bar, mark the spot where the unfortunate Richard Plantagenet, Duke of York, was slain in 1460, at the battle of Wakefield. Three or four trees formerly stood here, on the edges of a small triangular enclosure by the road-side. In 1865 only two remained. About 1866 one of them was blown down, leaving a solitary tree and the still living stump of the second, to keep up the remembrance. Camden says the enclosure was square, and that in it stood a cross. There is no cross existing there at the present time.

According to the *London Chronicle*, a famous ash tree was cut down in December, 1766, at East Newton, Yorkshire, which was supposed by good judges to be the largest and finest in the kingdom. It contained fourteen tons of good, sound, workable wood, and seven loads of top wood, &c. In February, 1828, an ash tree was cut down in Blackburn Hollows, near Shires Green, Yorkshire, containing 750 feet of solid timber. It was ten feet six inches across the stool.

In Hemsworth Churchyard is a fine old yew tree that a correspondent states will bear comparison with what may be seen of its kind at Fountains Abbey. If the visitor will give himself a little trouble to go from there to Brierley Common, two miles farther, he will there see a grand old oak.

Bierley Hall, near Bradford, Yorkshire, was the residence of Dr. Richardson, F.R.S., the eminent botanist, who planted here the first cedar of Lebanon in England, sent him by Sir Hans Sloane.

Some years ago a small yew tree was growing on the top of the tower of Hartshead Church, near Dewsbury, but it has since been removed to a more suitable place.

Swaledale. R. V. TAYLOR, B.A.

THE LARGEST OAK IN BRITAIN

IN spite of a rival claim put forward on behalf of an oak at Newland, in Gloucestershire, I believe that the largest oak in Britain — and our island home can boast of not a few of these giants of the greenwood, many of them famous, too, for their historical associations — stands in the parish of Cowthorpe, three miles from Wetherby, in the West Riding of the county of York.

The Cowthorpe Oak *(Quercus Sylvestris pedunculata)*, whose age has been computed to exceed 1,500 years, has, as may be supposed from its extraordinary size, been noticed in numerous works devoted to natural history and forestry. The circumference of its trunk, close to the ground, was, at the close of last century, according to Evelyn's " Sylva," seventy-eight feet. Shortly after the publication of that work, earth was placed around the base of the trunk, with a view to the preservation of the tree, which, by covering over some very considerable projections, reduced the girth of the stem at the ground line to sixty feet. In 1829, the Rev. Dr. Jessop measured the tree, and communicated its dimensions to Strutt's "Sylva

Cowthorpe Oak.

Brittanica." We transcribe the reverend doctor's details, which, he assures us, may be relied upon :—

Circumference at the ground	60 feet.
Ditto at the height of one yard	45 ,,
Height of the tree in 1829	45 ,,
Extent of the principal remaining limb	50 ,,
Greatest circumference of ditto	8 ,,

Dr. Jessop adds :—" The tree is hollow throughout to the top, and the ground plot inside (the account of which has been much exaggerated) may possibly afford standing-room for forty men."

In Loudon's " Arboretum " the diameter of the hollow within the tree, close to the ground, is given at nine feet ten inches.

"The circle occupied by the Cowthorpe Oak," says Professor Burnett, "where the bottom of its trunk meets the earth, exceeds the ground plot of that majestic column of which an oak is confessed to have been the prototype—viz., Smeaton's Eddystone Lighthouse."

In Burnett's "Outlines of Botany" we also read (vol. i. p. 59):—"So capacious is the hollow of the Cowthorpe Oak that upwards of seventy persons have been, as the villagers affirm, at one time therein assembled."

In the twelfth volume of Loudon's *Gardener's Magazine* (p. 588), the Cowthorpe Oak is said to be undoubtedly the largest tree at present known in England.

Shaw, in his "Nature Displayed," (vol. iii. pt. ii. p. 364), says:— "Many suppose the Cowthorpe Oak to be the Father of the Forest;" and in Kent's "Sylvan Sketches" (1825) mention is made of this oak as surpassing all others,

Tradition asserts that at one time the branches of this tree overshadowed half an acre of ground. A large branch which fell about the commencement of last century is said to have extended to a wall ninety feet from the trunk of the oak. On this wall, which still remains, the villagers, so the story runs, used to mount and pick the acorns from the overhanging branches. The leading or uppermost branch fell anterior to the date of any record concerning the tree. The manner in which it is said to have fallen is, however, remarkable. The main trunk having become hollow, the perpendicular shaft dropped down into the empty space and could never be removed. There it remained wedged in, doubtless tending to strengthen the hollow cylinder, and prevent concussion from the pressure of its enormous branches. In 1772 one of the side branches was thrown down in a violent gale of wind, and, on being accurately measured, was found to contain upwards of five tons of timber. The largest of the living branches at present extends over forty feet N.N.E. from the trunk. This giant limb is supported by a substantial prop.

A century ago Yorkshire children used to amuse themselves with a game called the "Dusty Miller." The Cowthorpe Oak was a meeting-place for this diversion. Through the rents in the shell of the trunk, then scarcely large enough to admit them, troops of merry village lads and lasses crept into the interior; and, provided with a spout, which was balanced in a hole in the wall of their living playhouse, they gathered the dry, crumbling dust and fragments of wood, and showered them over their companions outside.

In connection with this tree, an anecdote is related of that notable Yorkshireman, John Metcalfe, the sightless surveyor and road contractor, better known as "Blind Jack of Knaresborough." Jack was a frequent visitor to the tree, and would measure its girth correctly at any height within his reach, going round it with his long arms extended. He used to point out, too, with accuracy, by putting up his staff, the exact spot from which the great branch had fallen. Whenever he came, an old bloodhound which was kept near the tree, whose wont was to snarl at every stranger, fondled him and licked his hand. Blind Jack now lies at rest in Spofforth Churchyard, almost within sight of the old oak.

So great was the fame of the Cowthorpe Oak, that formerly small saplings raised from its acorns were sold in pots to visitors by the villagers for as much as a guinea each.

As the old oak now stands, it is a very picturesque object. It is situated in the centre of a small green paddock : hard by is the little village church, a very ancient structure, and the clear waters of the winding Nidd glide noiselessly past. The battered trunk, annually crowned with green foliage, is grand in its venerable decay. The old tree has been termed "the glory of England and the pride of Yorkshire;" and its enormous size, the growth of many centuries, entitles it to all the fame it has acquired.

In closing this brief account of the old tree, to which I have paid many a pleasant visit, I would point out that by far the most exhaustive treatment of the subject is that contained in a large quarto pamphlet, from the pen of Charles Empson, published in 1842. Copies of this work, which is entitled a "Descriptive Account of the Cowthorpe Oak," and contains an excellent plate of the tree, are now extremely scarce.

London   THOMAS B. TROWSDALE

HARDRAW FORCE

The North of England is richer than any other portion of the country in the beauty of its numerous waterfalls. The sublimity and grandeur of High Force and Cauldron Snout are our nearest approach to the Falls of Niagara. The Cataract of Lodore—"dashing and flashing and splashing and clashing," as it has done continually in the remarkable poem of Southey's for the last three score years or more, and will for evermore where the English language is spoken—is well known to every reader. Stock Ghyll Force, near Ambleside, has been often delineated by pen and pencil. The same may be said of the beautiful waterfall near Coniston Mines. "Dungeon Ghyll so foully rent," where "with ropes of rock and bells of air, three sinful sextons' ghosts are pent," in the verse of Coleridge.

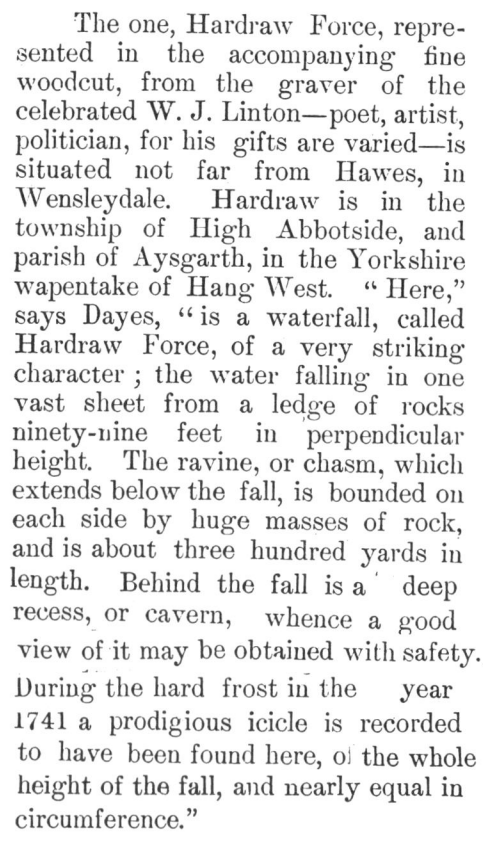

The one, Hardraw Force, represented in the accompanying fine woodcut, from the graver of the celebrated W. J. Linton—poet, artist, politician, for his gifts are varied—is situated not far from Hawes, in Wensleydale. Hardraw is in the township of High Abbotside, and parish of Aysgarth, in the Yorkshire wapentake of Hang West. "Here," says Dayes, "is a waterfall, called Hardraw Force, of a very striking character; the water falling in one vast sheet from a ledge of rocks ninety-nine feet in perpendicular height. The ravine, or chasm, which extends below the fall, is bounded on each side by huge masses of rock, and is about three hundred yards in length. Behind the fall is a deep recess, or cavern, whence a good view of it may be obtained with safety. During the hard frost in the year 1741 a prodigious icicle is recorded to have been found here, of the whole height of the fall, and nearly equal in circumference."

GEORGE MARKHAM TWEDDFLL, F.R.S.N.A.

THE PLUNDER OF A BATTLEFIELD

On the 14th of September, 1807, a leaden box containing 270 silver coins and some pieces of silver, the latter weighing about two pounds, was turned up by the plough in the parish of Bossall, in the county of York, at a farm occupied by Benjamin Wright, and belonging to Henry Cholmley, Esq., near the Lobster-house Inn, eight miles on the road from York to Malton. Most of the coins appear to have been struck at the Mint of St. Peter at York. From several coins of Alfred, Edward the Elder, and Athelstan having been found with St. Peter's penny, it is conjectured they were struck in the reigns of those monarchs, deposited in the treasury of the cathredal at York, in King Athelstan's time, and taken thence previously to the battle between Harold and the King of Norway, in 1066. They have the name of the master of the mint or of the city of York on the reverse, and are in perfect preservation, seeming almost fresh from the mint, and at all events cannot have been in much circulation, if any. From the contiguity of the spot where they were found to Stamford Bridge (about three miles), and from the above and following circumstances, as connected with history, it is almost manifest that this treasure was hidden soon after the memorable battle fought at Stamford Bridge, on the 23rd of September, 1066, between the great armies of Harold and the King of Norway, in conjunction with Tosti, Harold's brother, who had invaded the kingdom, and shortly before been in possession of York. It appears evident, from the pieces of silver found with the coins, that the whole was the plunder of a field of battle. Some of these appear separated or chopped off from others of them, and to be pieces of stirrups, others seem to have been ornaments for horses. There is also a small piece of a silver chain of coarse workmanship, which, no doubt, was either part of a bit or of the headstall of a bridle. In addition to these was a plain silver ring, curiously twisted at the joinings, with some broken ones, and a small silver crucifix. If there be weight in the above conclusion (and no other battle of adequate antiquity to the coins seems to have been fought in the neighbourhood), we may reasonably conjecture, from the fresh and perfect state of the money, that it had been plundered by the invaders from the mint at York when they obtained possession of the city, and that, after their defeat, it had been found upon their persons in the field of Stamford Bridge, as the spoil of battle, by one of the neighbouring rustics, sent to oppose William the Norman, who, in the midst of his rejoicings, he heard was already landed near Hastings. It is to be observed that the ground in which the above were found was on an unenclosed moor until about half-a-century ago, and had been once part of the forest of Gawtry; and it should not be omitted that there are some ancient foundations of a cottage within a few hundred yards of the spot. It is recorded that Harold claimed the whole of the spoil of this battle to himself, and did not properly reward his soldiers for their valour, which might induce some to bury the plunder to preserve it from his rapacity.

Bossal. R. BELT, JUN.

A YORKSHIRE PARISH COFFIN

IN Easingwold Church, Yorkshire, a few years back was (and I earnestly hope still *is*), carefully preserved, one of those now extreme rarities, a Parish Coffin, of which, at that time, I was able to obtain a drawing, and the requisite measurements. Of this interesting relic I give the following particulars, feeling sure that a record of so curious an object cannot be otherwise than acceptable to the readers of "Old Yorkshire."

The Coffin, carefully represented by the engraving on next page from a drawing especially made for me by Mr. J. H. Doe, has been strongly but somewhat roughly made of oak; has been clamped with iron, and its lid attached by hinges; and been so arranged as, evidently, when in use, to stand upon four legs as on a bier. It was, when not in use, kept in the west entrance to the church, under the tower, and was supported against the wall on strong iron staples. When the church was restored, the coffin was removed and placed in a corner of the bell chamber. Its inside dimensions, measured at the bottom, are, central length six feet seven inches; the length of the side from foot to shoulder, five feet three inches; the length of the side from the shoulder to the head, seventeen inches; the width across the shoulders, twenty-one inches; and the width at the foot nine inches. The sides are nine inches in height.

The lid was originally fixed to the coffin by three iron hinges on the right side of the body as it would lie for removal; one of the hinges being at the foot, another at the shoulder, and the third midway between the other two. The lid, which is somewhat larger than the coffin, (which it overlaps by about three-quarters-of-an-inch on the left side and at the head and foot,) has been split down the middle, and repaired by clamping the two halves together by means of five rough iron bands, one near the head, another near the foot, and the other three at intermediate distances between them. The corners and angles of the coffin itself have also been repaired, strengthened, and held together in the same manner by iron bands or plates; the iron in all cases being rough and so much corroded as to render it impossible to judge as to whether any kind of ornament was ever upon them. On the left side of the lid and coffin there have evidently, at one time, been fastenings, but these have long since disappeared. On each side the coffin at the distance of seven inches from the shoulder, is an iron ring and staple; the ring being about an inch-and-a-half in diameter, and another similar ring and staple is on each side about thirty inches from the feet. These two pair of rings, which balance the coffin well when lifted, were evidently intended for carrying it by, when brought into use.

That the coffin originally stood upon four legs is evident from the fact of there being four circular holes in the bottom—one at the head,

Parish Coffin, Easingwold Church, Yorkshire

one at the foot, and two others across the centre—in one of which are remains of a leg that had been broken off. From the others the legs had been taken away, or dropped out through age and decay. The coffin is of oak, very black with age, much decayed, and the wood very thin. It was thus spoken of in Gill's *Vallis Eboracensis*:—" Here is also preservd a large coffin, made of oak, with iron rings, of which the tradition is that it was once in general use as a kind of public bier for carrying the dead, with no other covering than the shroud, to the grave. It has, however, no marks of very high antiquity, or criteria by which its date can be ascertained." This note, I was informed by the then vicar of Easingwold, the Rev. Henry Ainslie, was written by his predecessor, the Rev. G. J. Allen. It was also noticed in these words in *Notes and Queries*, for 1852:—" In the Parish Church in Easingwold, in Yorkshire, there was within the last few years an old *oaken shell* or *coffin*, asserted to have been used by the inhabitants for the interment of their dead. After the burial the coffin was again deposted in the church."

The custom of having a coffin for general use provided by the parish although not general throughout the kingdom, obtained in many localities, and records of other examples than the one at Easingwold have come under my notice. One of the most interesting was communicated to me by my friend the Rev. Canon Hayman in these words:—" The old historical town of Youghal, in the County of Cork, has many features of interest for the antiquary, chiefest among which is the venerable Collegiate Church of St. Mary. The cemetery attached to this noble edifice is the *Pere la Chaise* of Ireland. The ground naturally forms a succession of terraces, here swelling into little knolls, there sinking into gentle declivities. A poet said of the Protestant burial ground at Rome 'It might make one in love with death to think that one should be buried in so sweet a place'; and the saying may be repeated of the Youghal churchyard. Death is here divested of its

Recess for Parish Coffin, Youghal Church Yard.

horror, and wears the softened aspect of stillness and unbroken repose. On its northern and western sides the cemetery is overhung by the old walls of the town, which are yet in good preservation. In a portion of those defences, nearly opposite to the western gable of the church, is a recessed, [coffin-shaped] aperture, of which a sketch is given on the accompanying engraving. Here, as old folk tell us, was kept the public coffin for the poor of Youghal. Whenever needed it was sent to the house of the dead; and so soon as it had discharged its office, it was replaced here. The walls, as may be perceived, are of three thicknesses. The newest piece, in front, is of hammered, well-squared masonry. More ancient is the furthest drawn, where the materials are less in size, and are less carefully finished. But, lying between these twain, is a fragment of a very old wall, built of exceedingly small stones, and evidently preserved from demolition because of its characteristic feature—the Parish Coffin Recess." The recess, as will be seen by the engraving, is coffin-shaped, with a stone at the bottom and another across the top, and in this the Parish Coffin stood upright when not in use, and could easily be lifted out when required for conveying a corpse from where it lay to the churchyard.

It is not necessary in this brief notice of the Easingwold relic, to enter at all into consideration of the subject of burial in shrouds or in any other manner either with or without coffins, but will be sufficient to state that interments without coffins were pretty general from early times downwards. The body being wrapped in cere-cloth, or in an ordinary shroud, was sometimes carried to the grave on a bier, or on some other temporary arrangement (for which a door taken off its hinges occasionally did duty), but in others, as in the instances to which I have called attention, a public coffin was provided by the parish for the use of its inhabitants. Even at the present day a somewhat analagous arrangement exists to my own knowledge in more than one Westmorland and Cumberland parish, of a parish hearse—*i.e.*, an appropriate carriage for the conveyance of the bodies of deceased members of the families of the parishioners,—being provided. The farmer, or whoever he is, in these outlying places, in case of a death occurring in his family, brings his own horse—or perchance a borrowed one—and yokes it to the hearse, which is kept in a building appropriate to the purpose, and takes it to where the body lies. It is then used for the funeral, and after the ceremony is over, is taken back to be ready for the next comer.

In the case of the parish coffin, or the bier being used, the body was carefully wrapped in a shroud, or swathed in cere-cloth; placed in the coffin for carrying to "God's Acre"; taken out when at the grave side; and lowered into the simple earth by the loving hands of those around. The tenantless coffin was then replaced in its receptacle, where it remained until some other sad occasion again brought it into requisition. Burial without coffins was not unfrequently made the subject of testamentary arrangement. For instance, in 1407, John de Burton, rector, of Aldwarke in Yorkshire, by his will ordered as follows:—"*Fest. S. Marg Virginis*, MCCCCVII. *Egó, Johannes de Burton, Rector medietatis Ecclesiæ S. Elenæ infra muros in vico de Aldwerk Ebor* . . . . . *Corpus meum Sepulturæ tradendum in loco per me nuper proviso, et pro sepulturâ corporis mei ordinato, ex parte australi chori dictæ Ecclesiæ, præcipiens et inhibens executoribus meis ne corpori meo cistam ligneam vel alia indumenta præparent, nisi tantum modo unum lintheamen pro corpore meo involvendo*"; which may be rendered thus:—" Feast of St. Margaret the Virgin, 1407. I, John de Burton, Rector of the moiety of the Church of St Helen, within the walls, in the village of Aldwerk, Yorkshire. . . . . . My body to be brought for burial unto the place lately provided by me, and set apart for the interment of my body, on the south side of the Choir of the said Church, [I] commanding and inhibiting my executors that they prepare not for my body a wooden coffin or other coverings, unless only one linen sheet to enwrap my body in."

In the "Table of Dutyes"—*i.e.*, fees—of Shoreditch church, 1664, are the amounts to be paid for burial without coffins; thus: "for a burial in ye new churchyard, without a coffin" eightpence; "for a burial in ye olde churchyard, without a coffin, seaven pence"; and "for the grave-making and attendance of ye Vicar and Clarke, on ye enterment of a corps uncoffined, the churchwardens to pay the ordinary duteys, and no more, of this table."

It would be interesting to know if other examples besides the one at Easingwold, occur in any of the churches of Yorkshire.

"*The Hollies,*" *Duffield, Derby.*   LLEWELLYNN JEWITT, F.S.A.

THE LEEDS CIVIC SCEPTRE

MANY of our readers may be unaware of the historical association which gathers round the mace or civic sceptre of the Leeds Corporation. It has a history which is both curious and interesting. It bears an engraved inscription, setting forth that it was the handiwork of a goldsmith named Maingee, "Arthur, Maingee de Leeds, fecit." This imposing emblem of municipal loyalty was made in 1694, and the goldsmith who made it paid the penalty of the law at the hands of the public executioner two years afterwards, having been convicted of high treason. The incidents connected with his trial and execution are very extraordinary, and might easily be woven by an imaginative mind into a most thrilling three-volume novel. The Leeds goldsmith was tried at the Summer Assizes held at York in 1696, before Lord Chief Justice Turton. He was charged with the crime of high treason, in counterfeiting the lawful coin of the realm. The principal witness against Maingee was an approver of the name of George Norcross, a supposed accomplice. In the Museum of the Leeds Philosophical Society are several of the implements used in the manufacture of the base coin. These were presented to the society by Mr. N. Scatcherd, F.S.A., of Morley, who has also left a long detailed account of Maingee's trial in manuscript. From this document we learn that the prosecution was conducted as much by the Chief Justice who tried the case as by the counsel for the prosecution. Norcross swore that he was employed by Maingee as a clipper, at 5s. a day, and that he saw him not only clip the sheets of base metal into the size or form of the intended shilling or half-crown, with shears, but that he also saw him stamp it on both sides by striking it heavily with a forge hammer, on a balk in the roof of his house, in a secret chamber. This witness was supported in his statement by a man and woman, whose stories were very incoherent. In summing up, his Lordship concluded thus :—" Gentlemen, if you believe what has been proved against Mr. Maingee to be true, you are to find him guilty. But, on the contrary, if you believe what Maingee and his witnesses tell you, and discredit the evidence for the King, you are to find him not guilty. But as far as I see, gentlemen, it appears otherwise. Still it is not I, but you, who must be his judge in this case. I have no more to say to you, gentlemen." We should fancy that his Lordship had said quite enough. The jury, of course, in obedience to such a charge, found the prisoner guilty, and Maingee was sentenced the same evening (26th August) to be drawn on a hurdle to the common place of execution, and there to be hanged as a traitor. Maingee's case was taken up by many friends, who appealed to the Government on his behalf, and he was actually twice reprieved. But the influence of the Chief Justice proved weightiest, and the unfortunate jeweller was executed on the 3rd of October following. In 1832, just 136 years after Maingee had suffered execution, it became necessary to pull down his old house in Briggate. The site of this house is about four doors below Mr. M'Kinnell's shop, at the corner of Kirkgate. In stripping off the roof of this old house, the workmen came upon a small secret chamber, and on the floor of this chamber they found two pairs of shears or clippers (now in the Museum), these being the very tools with which Norcross swore Maingee and himself used to clip the coins. After the lapse of nearly a century and a half, these two dumb witnesses corroborate the discredited evidence of this approver of infamous reputation. There are those, however, who yet question the guilt of Maingee. No discovery of dies, coins, base or otherwise, or any evidence of the room having been used as a workshop, must still leave the case in a questionable aspect.

Morley, near Leeds. THE EDITOR.

THE DUCKING STOOL AT MORLEY

THIS obsolete instrument of punishment was in use, where the Common Pound, or "Pinfold," was recently situated, but both the receptacle for stray cattle and the cure for brawling women have been swept away, and a public market now occupies the site; and where, now, itinerant vendors of quack medicines ply their trade, was formerly the "Ducking Stool"

Ducking Stool.

over a sheet of water, and such was the anxiety of our old villagers to keep up this old usage, that, when the ground was required for other purposes, this ancient instrument of punishment was removed to a suitable spot in Morley Hole, and subsequently to the Flush Pond, in Townend, near what was long known as "Ratten Row." Our ancestors, who considered the scold not only a domestic plague, but as a public nuisance, calculated to disturb the peace of the neighbourhood, and to interfere with the quiet of the common weal, endeavoured to stop these tongue batteries by means of the Ducking Stool,—

> "There stands, my friend, in yonder pool,
> An Engine called a Ducking Stool :
> By legal power commanded down,
> The joy and terror of the town.
> If jarring females kindle strife,
> Give language foul, or lug the coif,—
> If noisy dames should once begin,
> To drive the house with horrid din,—
> Away, you cry, you'll grace the stool ;
> We'll teach you how your tongue to rule."

This Ducking Stool appears to have been of Saxon origin, and consisted of a chair or stool, on which the offender was placed, and by the use of a long pole, was let down into a pool of water, as often as was desirable. We find from the following extract from an old poem on this subject, that the confirmed scold occasionally vented her angry clamour as soon as she recovered her breath after the first plunge, in which case, the immersion was repeated till exhaustion caused silence:—

> " Down in the deep the stool descends
> But here, at first, we miss our ends ;
> She mounts again and rages more
> Than ever vixen did before.
> If so, my friend, pray let her take
> A second turn into the lake ;
> And rather than your patience lose.
> Thrice and again repeat the dose.
> No brawling wives, no furious wenches,
> No fire so hot but water quenches."

We shall do our grand-dames an injustice if, before concluding this notice, we do not mention that the ducking stool was employed as a punishment not only for scolds and brawlers, but also for bakers and brewers, who either in the one case made bad bread or short weight, and in the other, sold ale in short measures or of bad quality.

Morley, near Leeds. THE EDITOR.

THE FLITCH OF BACON OATH

THE following has reference to a Flitch of Bacon Oath which was taken at Harrogate in 1764, and the ceremony is thus described in the *London Chronicle and Universal Evening Post* of July 3rd, 1764 :—

" York, 30th June, 1764.—Monday, the 25th inst., the following dinner, furnished by the gentlemen whose names stand opposite to the respective dishes, was given to Mr. and Mrs. Liddal, at the Green Dragon, in Harrowgate, on their taking the Flitch of Bacon Oath, inserted in the 607th Number (8th Vol.) of the *Spectator*. What was extraordinary in this couple was that so far from once repenting of their union within a year and a day (which is the time limited by the oath), they declared they could safely take it for the whole term they had been married, which is full 17 years :—

BILL OF FARE.

An entire flitch of bacon, by	Sir Thomas Clavering.
Beans for ditto	Major Whitmore.
Cabbage and colliflowers	Mr. Pemberton.
Three dozen of chickens	Mr. Liddal.
Two shoulders of mutton and cucumbers	Mr. Swin.
Two turbets	Capt. Lovell.
Rump of beef, &c., &c.	Capt. Powell.
Goose and plumbpudding	Capt. Bonner.
Quarter of lamb and salad	Mr. Barnard.
Tarts, jellies, strawberries, and cream	Mr. James.
Cherries, syllabubs, and blomonge	Capt. Townsend.
Leg of lamb and spinnage	Capt. Pearson.
Crawfish and pickled salmon	Capt. Fletcher.
Fry'd tripe and calves heads	Mr. Foord.
Gravy and pease soup	Capt. Sawer.
2 sucking pigs	Capt. Staveley.
Breast of veal ragood	Capt. Heron.
Ice cream and pine apples	Mr. Scott.
Surloin of beef	Mr. Blackett.
Pidgeons and green pease	Mr. Carr.
Lobsters and crabs	Mr. Douckery.
12 red herrings and 22 devils	Dr. Hunter, who could not attend.
Grace	Mr. Tomlinson,

The claret at dinner was charged to Lord Cardross, on Mr. Liddal taking the oath; and the malt liquors, &c., were set down in common to the company."

Horsforth. J. E. POPPLETON.

HORN-BLOWING AT RIPON

At Ripon a custom is retained which originated with the Saxons, and is perhaps one of the oldest in England. It is now discontinued, but it is an interesting relic of days of yore. Alfred the Great incorporated this city in 866; the regulation of the place was committed to the care of a wakeman, with a competent staff of elders and assistants, who instituted the horn-blowing service. An old writer describes the ancient ceremony as follows :—" It was, indeed, the custom of the Vizillarius or Wakeman to order that a horn should be blown every night at nine o'clock; and if any house or shop was broken open or robbed after that blowing of the horn, till the rising of the sun, why then the loss was obliged to be made good to the suffering inhabitant. For this obligation, or insurance, every householder used to pay fourpence a year; but if there was a back door to another street, from which double danger might be supposed, then it was to be eightpence.

The payment of the tax is discontinued, but the horn is still blown at the accustomed time. The horn-blower gives three long blasts before the residence of the mayor, and one blast at the Market Cross. The sound is rather dismal, but yet musical. It is a common cow's horn (with metal mouthpiece), curved in shape, measuring three feet six inches long. By means of a leathern strap across the bend of it, the horn is carried. The horn-blower carries his instrument in front of the mayor and corporation when they attend church. On April 2nd, 1846, died, at the age of eighty-two, a famous horn-blower named Benjamin Simmonds, who had occupied his appointment for thirty years. It is said he excelled all previous horn-blowers for the length and strength of blast.

The horn now used is not the original one; this is kept in the possession of the mayor, and Mr. Frank Buckland, who saw it in October, 1874, thus describes it:—" This ancient horn is not blown; it is handsomely mounted, and fastened on to a black velvet scarf, which is worn on the shoulders. At the juncture of the scarf with the horn are silver models of a miniature spur and crossbow. On the horn is this inscription :—' Antiquis et honorem et premia possi (I cannot quite construe this)—Vetustate 'lapsum restituit—J. Aiselbie, ARM., 1703.' On the lower part—' This horn was again restored, 1854, H. Morton, Mayor.' Attached to the velvet scarf are several silver plates. Every mayor on resigning office adds, or is supposed to add, a silver plate. I made a note of some of the dates, as follows :—1593, 1570, 1595, 1602, 1658. Some of the coats of arms and bosses are shaped like a sailor's hat. Several also are curious antique shapes. I was informed that the oldest badges are those of a Wakeman who lived in the time of Henry VIII., the name of one Gayscar, Wakeman in 1520, being marked especially."

Mr. William Harrison, late editor of the *Ripon and Richmond Chronicle*, told Mr. Buckland " that the horn itself is certainly of a date not later than the Conquest; that its form is true Saxon, and that there is another such shaped horn, made of ivory, preserved in the vestry of York Cathedral. This is the horn of Ulphas, who was prince of the western part of Deira. The Pusey horn is of the same peculiar elongated shape as the horns of York and Ripon, and illuminations in Saxon manuscripts frequently give representations of horns shaped like those at Ripon and York."

The name of Wakeman was exchanged for that of Mayor in 1604. Hugh Ripley was the last Wakeman and first Mayor.

The arms of the city are a golden horn with a black belt, ornamented with silver. The mouthpiece of the horn is turned to the dexter side of the shield.

Hull. WILLIAM ANDREWS.

THE STORY OF LITTLE JOHN

When the British Archæological Association met at Sheffield, in August, 1873, one of their excursions was to Wharncliffe Chase, where they were shown a bow which had been at Cannon Hall for 160 or 170 years, and which was supposed to have been the original bow of Little John, who was buried at Hathersage, in Derbyshire. The bow, some arrows, and a quantity of chain armour, were hanging at Hathersage Hall in the reign of Charles I. At the time of the Revolution, the estate of Hathersage came into the possession of a family of the name of Spencer, one of whom succeeded to the estate of Cannon Hall. About that time the bow and armour were removed to the latter place, and the armour was in existence there until about 70 years ago, when it was stolen by some workmen who were making repairs to the building. The bow bore the name of Col. Naylor, with the date 1715, and he was supposed to be the last man who ever strung it. It required a power of 160lbs. to draw the bow to its full! Only 90lbs. is the power which men of the present time use at archery meetings. The wood is now in so tender a condition that it is possible it would break if it were fully strung; but in 1715 the horn at both points was perfect, and Colonel Naylor shot a deer with it.

Little John (as he was jestingly called, from his being so much taller than his companions), or John the Nailer, the friend and companion of Robin Hood, was born somewhere in Derbyshire in the early part of the thirteenth century, and was brought up to the business of nail making, which trade he followed for some time, till his wonderful strength and prowess determined him to try his fortune elsewhere. Little is known of his career until the Battle of Evesham, in 1265, where he fought with the rebels under Simon de Montford, Earl of Leicester, who was defeated. Many of his followers, including Little John and Robin Hood, were outlawed.

Between these two distinguished heroes a great and lasting friendship commenced, and, owing to the difficulties in which they found themselves, they, with others of their defeated companions, retreated to the wood and fastnesses of the forest of Sherwood and the adjoining parts of Derbyshire and Yorkshire. Here they lived in the green woods a bold, free life, and were in one sense masters of the district to which they had attached themselves. Their exploits are well known; the Robin Hood Ballads having been printed and re-printed from generation to generation, and probably will be until time shall be no more.

When Robin Hood died, at the age of four score years, at his own request he was buried by Little John in Kirklees Park, Yorkshire, his native place, "with his bow in his hand, and a green sod under his head, another under his feet." After performing these last sad duties, Little John felt his own end approaching, and sought his native place.

It is reported that on his beholding the Vale of Hathersage, he said his career would soon be ended, and on arriving at a cottage near the church, he entered it, and soon after breathed his last.

The cottage, a rough stone structure, built without lime, we believe is now in existence, and the place where he is buried in the churchyard is still pointed out by the villagers. The grave is of great length—Little John is said to have been 6ft. 10in. in height—and is marked with a large stone at the head and foot. It is reported that some years ago the grave was opened, and several bones of large size were found, which were taken possession of by the explorer; but he afterwards suffered from so many unexpected misfortunes that he determined upon having them reburied, being urged thereto by men who had suffered in a similar manner. After the bones were replaced, their troubles, as the story goes, ceased.

Woodhouse.   F. BLACKETT.

A YORKSHIRE HIGHWAYMAN

NEAR the footpath on the road between Morley and Howley Hall is a square stone, sunk in the ground, bearing the words, scarcely legible now, "Here Nevison slew Fletcher, 1684." The story of this stone is, that Fletcher was a Howley man; that he tried to apprehend Nevison, and got him down at this spot, but that the thief shot Fletcher mortally, and so escaped. Nevison, as a thief and highwayman, made a deep impression upon the minds of the inhabitants of the districts which he visited, and his name is still remembered and familiarly spoken of in Howley, Morley, Brierley, Wakefield, and other places. He seems to have been popularly regarded as a thief of that attractive sort who robbed the rich and gave to the poor. He and his companions were horsemen, and committed their robberies chiefly between Newark and York. Nevison, whose Christian name was John, was a Yorkshireman. He was executed at York on 4th May, 1684. His famous ride to York is matter of history. About the latter end of Charles II.'s reign the robberies of Nevison had become so daring that Government was obliged to offer a considerable reward for securing him. In response to this offer, Fletcher attempted to apprehend him, when a struggle followed, in the course of which Nevison had recourse to a pistol, which, firing at the heart of Fletcher, he rolled from his body a lifeless corpse. Such is the story of a memorial which has for two hundred years excited the wonder and speculation of thousands of visitors from Leeds, Bradford, and other places, who have journeyed to the picturesque ruins of Howley Hall.

Morley, near Leeds   THE EDITOR.

SANDAL CASTLE

SANDAL CASTLE was built about the year 1320, by John Plantagenet, last Earl of Warren, as a seat for his mistress, Maude de Norford, the lady of the unfortunate Thomas, Earl of Lancaster. It was afterwards the property of Richard Plantagenet, Duke of York, who fell in the battle of Wakefield, in the year 1460. It afterwards became the residence of his son Richard, Duke of Gloucester, afterwards Richard III. It was demolished by the order of Cromwell in 1646. There are still some vestiges to mark the spot on which the castle stood. The following particulars concerning this ancient place, copied from Walpole's County of York, published in 1784, will, I have no doubt, be interesting to the readers of "Old Yorkshire":—"Queen Margaret, having marched into the north, raised an army of near 20,000 men, with

Sandal Castle.

which she intended, if possible, to deliver her husband, Henry VI., who had been some time a captive in the hands of the Yorkists. Her success was principally owing to the promises she made that such as attended her standard should be suffered to plunder the inhabitants south of the Trent, and such other places as they should subdue. The Duke of York, who was then at London, having heard of the Queen's design, was considerably alarmed, and therefore left the capital in order to prevent her further progress, ordering his son Edward to follow him with as many forces as he could raise. The Duke marched northward with the utmost expedition, but when he entered Yorkshire news was brought him that the Queen had raised a great army, so that he found himself under the necessity either of returning to London or engaging with a great disadvantage. Upon this he threw himself, by the advice of the Earl of Salisbury, into the Castle of Sandal, where he thought he could be safe till the arrival of his son, as the Queen had no artillery, which at that time was coming into use. The Queen, who was both cunning and courageous, concealed some of her men behind an eminence, and with the remainder attacked the Castle, threatening the Duke in the most abusive and insulting manner, and by that artifice Richard was led into the snare ; for, not imagining she had any more men than those with her, he ventured out, and a most bloody battle ensued. The Duke, finding his army surrounded by the enemy, rushed into the thickest part of the ranks, and was killed, after he had displayed such courage as would have done honour to one of the old Roman generals. This battle was fought on the 30th day of December, 1460, and the dead body of the Duke being brought to the Queen, she ordered the head to be cut off and fixed on one of the gates of York city."

The scenery around the Castle is beautiful and picturesque. From a mound close to the ruins splendid views are obtained of the immediate neighbourhood and places at a great distance. The ruins are approached from a rather romantic lane, called Cock and Bottle Lane, from its having a public house in it known as the Cock and Bottle Inn. An ash tree in the fence of the field in which the remains of Sandal Castle are situated is a remarkable specimen of antiquity. In several places the roots of this noble-looking tree are quite bared, and form a natural flight of steps, by means of which the visitor ascends several feet, and then mounts over some wooden rails ere the enclosure is entered. The mound is known by the name of " Sandal Castle Hill," and is artificial, being composed principally of clay, granite stones, and earth. It was raised when the Castle was besieged in the time of civil war, in order to protect the building from the cannon of the besiegers, who had taken up a commanding position on Lawe Hill, Wakefield, upon which they, too, had raised a mound, which is also still in existence. It is said the Sandal mound was made in one night. The Castle, however, was exposed on that side of it which faced Horbury ; and at a place afterwards called " Castle Hill," in that township, the Parliamentarians threw up a temporary hill, placed cannon upon it, and commenced firing at the castle before the besieged were aware of what the besiegers had done and accomplished in that direction. They thus effected a breach in the walls. The first cannon ball that entered the building was fired from the hill at Horbury, and this advantage being followed up, led to the surrender of the fortress to the Parliamentarians after a very obstinate resistance on the part of its Royalist defenders. A man named Whitehead, holding the situation of parish clerk at Horbury Church, was the cannonier who fired the first shot that struck and damaged the Castle. This man never left his duty at the cannon until the siege was finished, and his wife daily carried him his rations from the village. The family of Whitehead, before and after his time, for several generations, had one of its members officiating as clerk at Horbury Church. Many relics of this siege have been picked up in adjoining fields, which were formerly parts of Sandal Castle Park. The hill made at Horbury for the occasion was much larger than the mound at the top of Lawe Hill, and apparently at a nearer distance to the Castle. This hill was situated on a piece of table or sort of platform land, very suitable for the purpose it was then used for, and in a most commanding position as regarded the operations against the Royalists. It was in existence a long time after the destruction of Sandal Castle, but, having come into the ownership of Mr. Schofield, solicitor, of Horbury, that gentleman caused the earthwork, &c., to be removed. The site, however, is still known as "Castle Hill," and has been famous for having on it a well, called "Castle Hill Well."

I have in my possession a cannon ball found in 1814, in a field near Sandal Castle ruins, by a Mr. Walsh, landlord of the Cock and Bottle Inn. It is made of wrought iron, and weighs about six pounds. A short time since several persons, out of antiquarian curiosity, dug up a portion of the top of Sandal Castle Hill, and discovered what appeared to have been part of the stone work of a watch tower of the castle. It is clear from this circumstance that one side of the mound was quite close against the Castle walls. Some kind-hearted persons at one time, for the use of visitors, erected a wooden seat upon the hill, but it has disappeared.

Year by year these interesting remains of Sandal Castle grow less and less. What with the ruthless hand of time, which makes no distinction, crumbling them by degrees to dust, and overzealous admirers breaking small pieces of stone off the old walls, and taking them away as articles of curiosity, as well as stormy winds and rains at times beating against them in full force, there is no wonder at this. No one seems willing to restore the old fabric. Praise,

Ruins of Sandal Castle.

however, is due to Sir Lionel Pilkington, the owner, for allowing them to stand as they are; and the gratification they afford to visitors is far beyond description. The walls appear in some places to have been several yards in thickness, the outsides being faced with good stones cramped together with irons, and the middle portions filled up with all kinds of stones well cemented. What appears to have been a large window place is faced with excellent and large stones. Thousands of spectators at different periods have mounted this place, and many persons have cut their initials on the walls.

From the mound the course of the river Calder is seen to advantage. The chain bridge at Thornes attracts the eye, and the serpentine course of the stream is seen. The Calder flows from the west, and from the Thornes Chain Bridge towards the castle ruins. Then abruptly a bend is formed, and the current flows westerly a certain distance; but, by a circuitous route, it changes its course again, and appears to return towards Sandal. On nearing the Calder Soap Works it turns round towards Wakefield. From Lupset Pastures to this point, in order to avoid these bends in the river, a short canal has been made, which much facilitates the navigation of the Calder by the numerous vessels passing to and fro, laden with grain, coal, stone, &c. An extensive piece of ground which lies betwixt these bends of the river is called the "Pugneys," and sometimes the "Pugnals," and some of the adjoining fields are also known by that singular designation; and, being near to the site of Sandal Castle, it is generally believed that the hottest and fiercest part of the "Battle of Wakefield Green," on the last day of December, 1460, was fought on these grounds. Lame Hill, Holmfield House, Lupset Hall, Thornes House, Carr Lodge, Christ Church, South Ossett, Trinity Church, North Ossett, St. James's Church, Horbury, Woolley, Edge, &c., as well as the whole town of Wakefield, are distinctly seen amongst the "thousand and one" interesting objects which command the attention of the beholder.

The Duke of York, at the time of his defeat on Wakefield Green, was the owner of Sandal Castle, and also the lord of the extensive manor of Wakefield, which reached thirty-four miles in length, from Normanton to the borders of Lancashire. Sandal Castle at that period was the chief manor house of that important feudal territory; hence the Duke's reasons for garrisoning it in the time of the Civil War, with his followers.

Ossett. JOHN HEWITT.

A TOWN OF MANY NAMES

INCLUDING Facelac of the Domesday Survey and its present name, Filey has had thirteen names during the last 800 years, or a new name every 61 years, and the present name Fi(ve)ley, is simply an abbreviation, and means five meadows. It has been called by the different appellations of File, Fieling, Fielay, Fyley, Fively, Fiviley, Fyveley, Fiveleiam, Finelay, Philaw, and Filo—in all, thirteen names or modes of spelling. Filey is famous for lobsters, and Flamborough for crabs. Ralph, the son of Ralph de Neville, gave the stone in his quarry here towards building the monastery at Bridlington. Roger, the son of Vetre de Gristhorpe, in 1175, gave four acres of land in the field of Gristhorpe, with one messuage, &c., for the finding of lights in the house of Fountains, where the poor and strangers then lay. The church is dedicated to St. Oswald, who was King of Northumbria, taken prisoner, and torn limb from limb by the pagan Penda, King of Mercia, at Oswaldestre, praying for his murderers. The church stands in the North Riding, and the village stands in the East Riding. The church is a cruciform building, 131 feet by 71 feet, and is a cathedral in miniature,

THE LIFE OF AN ENGLISH MONASTERY

IN the story of the life of one of our ancient abbeys a many-sided tale has to be told. If we look from the present to the past, we are too apt to view the mouldering ruins with an over-sympathetic eye. The glamour of a strange story is cast over us. Our mental restoration of the old ruins to our fancy of the reality is too apt to be, if not of "the dim religious light," of the more sensuous type that a strong imagination raises from a fleshy basis.

It is not to the present purpose to trace the ethical life of a community of monks; it is only intended to give some prominent glimpses of their mundane existence from the cradle to the grave of their house. In order to do so, I will take the story of one of the most conspicuous ruins, frequented alike both for scenic beauty and for architectural display—an ancient establishment having one of the most unique beginnings and favourable careers in the history of English monasteries—the story of the Cistercian Abbey of St. Mary of Kirkstall.

The first remark generally made by visitors to our ruined abbeys is to the effect that the monks of old were admirable judges of landscape beauty, and sybarite followers of the fatness of the land.

As a rule, the country surrounding one of these abbeys presents a charming picture of leafy magnificence, rolling down or woodclad crag, at the foot of which flows some shimmering river or rippling brook, while under the very feet an expanse of cultivated meadow and upland speaks of a long continuance of agricultural prosperity. The error of this conclusion is largely attributable to the topographers who have written what little may have been written on the subject of the place which they visit. In the case of Kirkstall, for instance, who, after reading Dr. Whitaker's pompous encomium—" Amongst the monastic remains of the north of England, Kirkstall may claim the second place, whether it be considered as a feature in a landscape or a specimen of architecture. In the former view it must, perhaps, yield the palm to Bolton; in the latter indisputably to Fountains"—would guess its beginning, of which we have an almost photographic view in the contemporary account of the foundation?

As we have already stated, a miraculous intervention is the preface to the story. Some monks from the Abbey of Fountains had in 1147 obtained from Henry de Laci, Baron of Pontefract, the most potent and opulent man in the north of England, grandson of Ilbert de Laci, a mighty leader under the Conqueror, the grant of the town of Barnoldswick, in Craven, for the purpose of establishing a Cistercian monastery. Henry de Laci was then lying dangerously ill, and his gift was a propitiation for his sins and sufferings. At Barnoldswick the pious brethren happened to come to litigation with the secular priest and the laity by reason of a little overbearing and unjustifiable conduct, which had to be referred to Rome for settlement. In one of his journeys, evidently to Pontefract, the seat of his patron, Abbot Alexander happened to pass down Airedale, to Leeds, no doubt, as one of his stages, when, in a secluded part of the township of Headingley, then subinfeudated by De Laci to William Patefyn, he is said to have discovered some pious anchorites who had taken up their abode in a very out-of-the-way corner of the township, by the river-side. Of course he asked them their manner of living, the form of their religion, and whence they came. Seleth, one of them who appeared to be the leader, answered—

<small>I was born in the southern part of this kingdom. A revelation from heaven having been made to me I came hither, for when I was in the land of my nativity a voice came to me during sleep saying, "Arise, Seleth, and go into the province</small>

Cistercian Canon.

of York, and search diligently for a valley which is called Airedale, and a certain place which is called Kirkstall, and there provide a future habitation for brethren to serve my Son." He asked from whom the voice came, and the answer was, "I am Mary, and my son is Jesus the Nazarene, Saviour of the world." Awaking I considered what I should do concerning this revelation, and then casting my hope on the Lord, lett my home and domesties and hastily departed, doubting nothing; she who called me leading me to this valley, which thou seest I have not reached without difficulty. But first I learnt from the shepherds and herdsmen that this place in which we now dwell was called Kirkstall.

This is a bit of pious misrepresentation on the part of brother Seleth, for the name Kirkstall—the church-stead—was only coined after the church had been founded, as is admitted; and which has called forth the indignation of the virtuous of later ages, it did not apply to the wilderness where Seleth had taken up his abode. However—

I was alone for many days, eating roots and herbs, and the alms which Christian people of their charity gave to me. Afterwards those brethren whom thou now seest joined themselves to me, having me for ruler and master. We live after the form of the brethren of Le Ruth, having nothing personal to ourselves either in meat or clothing, seeking all things by the labour of our hands.

Hearing this, Abbot Alexander began to think within himself of the site and circumstances of the place, of the pleasant valley and the water then flowing through it, and of the adjacent woods for the erection of our buildings; and he saw that the place was sufficiently suitable there to build an abbey; and, like an astute priest, he soon turned the matter to his own advantage. He began to advise the hermit brethren as to the health and profit of their souls, proposing to each the peril of his own will, the poverty of the community, their being disciples without a master, laity without a priest, persuading them of the greater perfection and better form of his religion. He then bade them good-bye, went straight to Henry de Laci, and begged the place over their heads. It so happened that the gift had to be confirmed by William Patefyn, the sub-in-feudatory, with whom De Laci was at variance, as were many Lords and their feudal tenants; for we must not forget all this was happening in the troublous reign of Stephen, when master and man were often at daggers drawn. But the monk was equal to the occasion, and he improved it. Henry de Laci called William to him, obtained his assent to the gift, and then "the bickerings and discords that had existed between them ceased, and they were made friends from that day;" and the place occupied by these hermits, with the adjacent wood and water according to certain boundaries, passed "to God and to the monks," they paying a rent to William and his heirs of five marks.

Having thus secured a more commodious place, Alexander began to build a church (*basilicam*) in honour of Mary, always virgin; and the offices having been erected, he changed the name and called the monastery Kirkestall. On the 14th Kalends June (19th May), 1152, the colony at Barnoldswick departed to their new home, "which is now called Kirkstall, a place of groves, unfruitful of crops, a place nearly destitute of good things, except wood and stone, and a pleasant valley, with the waters of a river flowing through it." Henry de Laci, with his own hand, laid the foundation-stone of the church, and found the money to build it; on which account Kirkstall yet remains an almost unique specimen of a large conventual church built as a whole, and not in portions at various times. It was, however, in the reign of Henry II. that the offices were erected in stone, viz., the dormitories of the monks and *conversi*, the refectory, the cloisters, and the chapter-house; and all these were covered with tiles in the best fashion. It is said that the church and the above buildings occupied a period of thirty years in construction. De Laci was, indeed, a munificent patron. In addition to his other great gifts, he gave half a mark of silver out of the rent of "Cliderhou" for a lamp to be burnt day and night in the presence "sacro sancti corporis Domini," and he is said to have been buried in the church that he had founded; but upon that a doubt must rest, for the monkish chronicler of the house says "nescitur ubi sepultus fuit, creditur quod ipse in terra sancti obiit vij Kalendas Octobris." He is known to have been succeeded by his son Robert de Laci, who died on the 12th Kal. September, 1193, and buried, according to the chronicler, at Kirkstall, "cum epitaphio;" but what that was we are not told.

Among the witnesses of the charter of foundation we have names that throw some light upon the social condition of the valley. William de Hedingleia is William Patefyn, of Headingley; in Lambert (Medicus) the doctor, Arnold the priest, Gamel the son of Besing, we apparently have natives of lowly condition. There is no mention of Seleth, who should have been a prominent man, had he been such a reality as the legend makes him to be; but in Henry Hathecrist we have a person whose individuality it is not good to determine. Is it possible that he could have been a "hot-gospeller" and a member of the band of anchorites?

Norman Doorway, Kirkstall Abbey.

The warmth of the religion of these enthusiasts is given graphically in a word-portrait of one of the early Abbots—Turgesius (? a Latinisation of Tor, a man of Danish descent), a man of singular abstinence and most severe chastiser of his body, being always clothed in sackcloth, to suppress the unlawful motions of the flesh by harsh clothing carrying in his mind these words of the gospel, "They that wear soft clothing are in King's houses." His garment at all times was but one

Kirkstall Abbey.

cowl and one tunic, without any addition; yet he had no more in winter and no less in summer. Thus he yielded to neither season, so that you would neither think him to be chilled with the cold nor inflamed with the heat. In the dead of winter, when the sharpness of the cold was most vehement, he never took care for any defence against the hardness of the weather; he would not wear socks upon his feet, nor permit straw to be laid for him to lie on. He stood at the night watches, when one having double garments on was almost frozen stiff, as if he felt no uneasiness, and we say that he repelled the cold of the season with the ardour of the inward man. No man pleasanter than he, none more temperate; he never tasted wine unless in those parts where no other drink can be found. There is no need to talk of flesh; fish he permitted to be set before him, for the sake of those who sat by him, only to look at, not to eat. He was frequently weeping, and in compunction when discoursing he seldom refrained from tears; never at the office of the altar without devotion; never said mass without tears, whereof he shed so great a flood that he did not seem to weep but to rain down tears, insomuch that the sacerdotal vestments he wore could scarce be used by any other. After spending nine years at Kirkstall, Turgesius resigned and returned to Fountains where he died.

The austerity that he practised did not long prevail at Kirkstall. The convent fell into woeful debt, infinitely more and more distressing than that of St. Edmund's, Bury, upon which Carlyle dilates with so much pathos in his account of that worthy Abbot Samson in "Chartism, Past and Present." According to the state of the house on the day of St. Lambert, bishop and martyr, 1284, the time of the creation of Abbot Hugh de Grimston, the convent only possessed 16 draught oxen, 84 cows, 16 yearling and young bullocks, 21 asses and no sheep, although the raising of sheep had always been a great feature of the Cistercian economy. The debts certainly due by a recognisance made before the Barons of the Exchequer were £4,402 12s. 7d.; by written bonds there were due to James de Fistolis (mark him Shylock!) 500 marks; to the Abbot of Fountains, 50 marks; 59 sacks of wool and 9 marks were due to Barnard Talde; besides the acquittances in the hands of John Saclden (? Shackleton a name yet well known in the neighbourhood) for 340 marks. The total of this monstrous burden was £5,248 15s. 7d., besides the 59 sacks of wool, a sum which cannot have represented less than £150,000 of present money. Of course this was utter bankruptcy. The convent, which had been in difficulties since the reign of Henry III., whose Royal protection they had to seek, was compelled to again resort to the King to obtain by his interposition an extension of time for satisfying the legal claims made upon them; and they obtained it. Abbot Hugh, who seems to have been a man well qualified to wrestle with these burdens, shows his brethren the deplorable state of the house, and in the end he managed to get the affairs within control. In 1301, before his death, which occurred in 1304, the effects and debts of the house, as proved at the visitation on the Sunday next before the feast of St. Margaret the Virgin, were—draught oxen 216, cows 160, yearlings and bullocks 152, calves 90, sheep and lambs 4,000. The debts of the house were but £160; and to this most satisfactory statement Richard, Abbot of Fountains, affixed his seal. Of Hugh de Grimston, evidently a man of middle-class parentage, perhaps a monk, and most likely son of one of the tenants of the abbey, it may, indeed, be said, "Well done, thou good and faithful servant!"

From this period, for the two hundred and odd years of its continued existence, a life of tranquility amounting to torpidity, settled upon the abbey.

The abbey was surrendered on the 22nd November, 1540, and the deed of surrender gives us a good description of it at that date. The site of the late monastery, with apple orchards, gardens, and the cemetery and other places within the precincts, contained by estimation 6 acres; a meadow close, called Brewhouse close, containing 6 acres; another meadow, then called Overkirkgarth, containing 5 acres; a pasture field, called Pente's Close, containing half an acre; another pasture close behind the stable, then called Colman Croft, containing $2\frac{1}{2}$ acres and two water corn mills within the site. Stevens fills up the details and makes a picture of cosy comfort, refreshing in its serenity after a glimpse of the busy activity pervading the neighbourhood of to-day.

Adorned with gardens, dovecotes, etc., and whatever was either for use or ornament, and all conveniently seated on the banks of a delicate river, calm and clear, which perhaps has contributed to the general misnomer of the place, which is frequently called Christall, instead of Kirkstall—it is locally pronounced Kerstle to this day—not only by the vulgar, but by some persons of more liberal education, and by that name printed in the best maps that were ever made for the county.

Leeds   W. WHEATER.

LONGEVITY IN WHITBY

Whitby and its neighbourhood appear to be very favourable to health and length of days, as instanced in the longevity of many of the inhabitants. Upon examining the tombstones and burial-registers, we find the ages of 70 and 80 are common, from 80 to 90 very frequent, and several attained the age of 100 or upwards. Philip Lawson died at Whitby in June, 1833, aged 104 years; Ann Brown died here in June, 1852, aged 101. From seventy to eighty years back, Joseph Stonehouse died here, aged 108; Margaret Cooper, aged 100; and Margaret Ingham, aged 103. During the year 1857 there were interred in Whitby 250 bodies, of which twenty-two died between the ages of 50 and 60, thirty between 60 and 70, forty-one between 70 and 80, fifteen between 80 and 90, and five above 90 years. Mrs. Bambles, of Whitby, died in 1812, aged 94 years. She lived in the same house with two sisters, one older, the other younger than herself, both of whom were alive at the time of her decease. The eldest was an unmarried lady, who had great vivacity of spirits, and frequently distinguished herself from her sisters, both of whom were widows, by the epithet of the "young maid." Thos. Brignell, of Whitby, died in 1796, aged 96. He was for many years an eminent whitesmith and mechanician, and was well known in most of the ports of England, especially in those trading to the Baltic and Greenland seas, for the excellence of his screws and harpoons. Along with Mr. Wilson, another mechanic of Whitby, he appears to have constructed the first locomotive carriage, but on what principle we have no information. The invention, however, came to nothing; probably it was too much in advance of the age in which it was produced. Francis Ellis, mariner, of Whitby, died in 1771, aged 95; within a few days, also, died Mary, his wife, aged 93 years. Henry Wells, of Whitby, died in 1794, aged 109. His health was uniformly sound and good till a short time before his death. He was, however, almost blind, and was led through the streets by a poor woman, carrying on his shoulders for sale a few mats of his own manufacture. William Wilson, of East Row, near Whitby, died in 1795, aged 100 years. In the adjoining parish of Sneaton, Jane Sedman, died in February, 1792, aged 111; and in July of the same year, William Sedman, her husband, died, aged 116. This ancient pair lived together ninety years as man and wife. In 1710 Margaret Robinson died at the same place, aged 102; and in 1736 Mary Wilkinson, at the age of 101; and from 1743, to the beginning of the present century, twenty-one persons died there aged from 80 to 90, and twenty-two between 90 and 100 years old. Joseph Thompson, of Lythe, near Whitby, died in 1817, aged 102 years. In 1825 John Sedman, of Ugthorpe, died, aged 100 years. His father attained the same great age. Dorothy Burley, of Ruswarp, died in 1826, aged 100 years and 2 months; Francis Knaggs, of Sleights, died in 1828, aged 105; William Sneaton, of Aislaby, died in the same year, aged 103; and Isaac

Dobson, of Mickleby, died in 1829, aged 100 years and 9 months. Mrs. Harrison, who was born at Whitby, and had lived there all her life, celebrated her 100th birthday September 10th, 1873. After a drive out, she was joined at tea by her brother from Scarborough, who was 90 years of age. Her faculties were unimpaired. Her sister, who lived at Burniston, near Scarborough, and was 97 years of age, would have joined this remarkable family gathering, had not her friends at the above place been busy with the harvest.

Richmond. R. V. TAYLOR, B.A.

HENRY JENKINS

THE oldest Yorkshireman of whom we have any record is Henry Jenkins; some say the oldest Englishman; others, the oldest man in the world since the days of the Hebrew patriarchs. He was born at Ellerton-upon-Swale, a small village in the North Riding of this county, one mile from Catterick, and six from Richmond, in the year 1500, and the Parish Register of Bolton-on-Swale records his death December

9th, 1670, thus showing that he had completed his 169th year. The proofs on which the great age of Jenkins rest have been examined and sifted with the greatest severity and care, in order, if possible, to detect the slightest fallacy : but the fact appears to be established beyond the reach of reasonable doubt. Belonging to a humble station in society, but few events of his life are recorded, beyond his extraordinary longevity. His youth was passed in the laborious employments of agriculture ; afterwards he became butler to Lord Conyers, of Hornby Castle ; in his old age he used to earn a livelihood by thatching houses and fishing in the rivers.

The earliest and most reliable account of Jenkins is given by Mrs. Anne Savile, daughter of John Savile, Esq., of Methley, ancestor of the Earls of Mexborough, a lady whose testimony may be considered as above suspicion, in a letter to Dr. Tancred Robinson, F.R.S.[*] published in the Transactions of the Royal Society :—This lady says, "When I first came to live at Bolton, it was told me that there lived in that parish a man near one hundred and fifty years old ; that he had sworn as a witness in a cause at York, to one hundred and twenty years, which the judge reproving him for, he said he was butler at that time to Lord Conyers ; and they told me it was reported his name was found in some old register of Lord Conyers' menial servants. Being one day in my sister's kitchen, Henry Jenkins coming in to beg an alms, I had a mind to examine him, I told him he was an old man, who must soon expect to give an account to God of all he did or said ; and I desired

Henry Jenkins.

---

[*] Dr. Tancred Robinson was second son of Thomas Robinson, Esq , and own brother to Sir William Robinson, Baronet, of Newby-on Swale. He was M.D., and F.R.S., and was knighted on his appointment as Physician to King George I.

him to tell me, very truly, how old he was; on which he paused a little, and then said, to the best of his remembrance he was about one hundred and sixty two, or one hundred and sixty-three. I asked him what kings he remembered. He said, 'Henry VIII.' I asked him what public thing he could longest remember. He said, 'Flodden Field.' I asked him whether the King was there. He said, 'No; he was in France, and the Earl of Surrey was general.' I asked how old he might be then. He said between ten and twelve, 'for,' says he, 'I was sent to Northallerton with a horse-load of arrows; but they sent a bigger boy from thence to the army with them.' I thought by these marks I might find something in histories; and looking into an old chronicle, I found that Flodden Field was about one hundred and fifty-two years before, so that if he was ten or eleven years old, he must be one hundred and sixty-two or one hundred and sixty-three, as he said, when I examined him. I found that bows and arrows were then used, and that the Earl he named was then General, and that King Henry VIII. was then at Tournay: so that I don't know what to answer to the consistencies of these things, for Henry Jenkins was a poor man, and could neither write nor read. There were also four or five in the same parish that were reputed, all of them, to be one hundred years old, or within two or three years of it, and they all said he was an elderly man ever since they knew him, for he was born in another parish, and before any register was in churches, as it is said.* He told me then, too, that he was butler to Lord Conyers, and remembered the Abbot of Fountains Abbey very well, who used to drink a glass with his lord heartily; and that the dissolution of the monasteries he well remembered."

The following remarks are from the pen of Dr. Tancred Robinson, Physician to King George I.:—"This Henry Jenkins died December 8th, 1670, at Ellerton-on-Swale. The battle of Flodden Field was fought on the 19th September, 1513. Henry Jenkins was twelve years old when Flodden Field was fought; so that he lived one hundred and sixty-nine years. Old Parr lived one hundred and fifty-two years and nine months; so that Henry Jenkins outlived him, by computation, sixteen years, and was the oldest man born on the ruins of the post-diluvian world. This Henry Jenkins, in the last century of his life, was a fisherman, and used to wade in the streams. His diet was coarse and sour; but towards the latter end of his days he begged up and down. He was sworn in Chancery, and other courts, to above one hundred and forty years' memory, and was often at the Assizes at York, whither he generally went afoot; and I have heard some of the country gentlemen affirm that he frequently swam in the rivers after he was past the age of one hundred years."

Mrs. Savile having sent a copy of her statement respecting Jenkins to Sir Richard Graham, of Norton Conyers, near Ripon, which was inserted in the household book of that family, a transcript of it was

---

* Parish Registers were first ordered to be kept in 1538.

afterwards given to Roger Gale, the celebrated antiquary, by Sir Reginald Graham, accompanied with the following note from himself :—
"Sir,—I have sent you an account of Henry Jenkins, as I find it in my grandfather's Household Book,—the time of his death is mentioned, under the letter as I have set it down; it seems not to have been the same hand: he must have lived sometime after Mrs. Savile sent this account to Sir Richard. I have heard Sir Richard was Sheriff when Jenkins gave evidence to six score years, in a cause between Mr. How and Mrs. Wastell, of Ellerton. The Judge asked him how he got his living, he said 'by thatching houses and fishing.' This letter is without date, but appears to have been written by Mrs. Savile in the year 1661, or 1662, by what she says of the time when she examined the old man, compared with that of Flodden Field, and was eight or nine years before he died, for I found his burial in the Register of Bolton Church, thus:—'December the 9th, 1670, Henry Jenkins, a very old poor man.' And was also shewed his grave.—R. GRAHAM, Norton, 26th August, 1739-40."

From his extraordinary age he was often summoned as a witness, to give evidence on ancient rights and usages, where his evidence was frequently of the most material importance. "A Commission out of the Court of Exchequer, dated 12 Feby., 19 Charles II., authorizing George Wright, Joseph Chapman, John Burnett, and Richard Fawcett, gents, to examine witnesses, as well on the part of the plaintiff as defendant, in a tythe cause between Charles Anthony, vicar of Catterick, complainant, and Calvert Smithson, owner and occupier of lands, in Kipling, in the parish of Catterick: Depositions taken in the house of John Stairman, at Catterick, co Ebor, on the 15th April, 1667 :— Henry Jenkins, of Ellerton-upon-Swale, labourer, aged one hundred and fifty-seven, or thereabouts, swore and examined, says—'That he has known the parties seven years, and that the tithes of lambs, calves, wool, colts, chickens, goslings, pigs, apples, pears, plums, flax, hemp, fruit, and multure of mills were paid in kind, by one Mr. Calvert,* the owner of the lordship or manor of Kipling, to one Mr. Thriscroft,† above threescore years since, the Vicar of Catterick; and were so paid in kind during the time of the said Mr. Thriscroft's continuance; and, after, the tithes of Kipling were paid in kind to one Richard Fawcett, deceased, for many years together as vicar of Catterick; and that this deponent never knew of any customary tithes, paid by any of the owners or occupiers of the lordship or manor of Kipling, or any other of the towns or hamlets within the said parish of Catterick; but all such particulars named in the interrogatories were ever paid in kind to the vicar there for the time being."‡

---

* George Calvert, Esq., afterwards created Baron Baltimore.
† Henry Thriscroft was Vicar of Catterick from 1594 till 1603; Richard Fawcett, from 1603 till 1660.
‡ Clarkson's History of Richmond, p. 396.

At the Assizes at York, in 1655, Jenkins appeared as a witness to prove a right of way over a man's ground; he swore to one hundred and twenty years' memory; for that time he remembered a way over the ground in question. Being cautioned by the Judge to beware what he said, as there were two men in the court above eighty years of age each, who had sworn they remembered no such way, he replied that those men were boys to him. Upon which the Judge asked those men how old they took Jenkins to be. They answered that they knew him very well, but not his age, for he was a very old man when they were boys.

In the cause mentioned in Sir Reginald Graham's letter, between How and Wastell, of Ellerton, Jenkins again gave evidence to one hundred and twenty years' memory. One of the Judges asked him what remarkable battle or event had happened in his memory, to which he answered that when the battle of Flodden Field was fought, where the Scots were beat with the loss of their King, he was turned of twelve years of age. Being asked how he lived, he said by thatching and salmon fishing; that when he was served with a subpœna he was thatching a house, and he would " dub a hook " with any man in Yorkshire. He also stated that he had been butler to Lord Conyers, of Hornby Castle, and that Marmaduke Brodelay, Lord Abbot of Fountains, did frequently visit his lord, and drank a hearty glass with him— that his lord often sent him to enquire how the lord abbot did, who always sent for him to his lodgings, and after ceremonies (as he called it) passed, ordered him, besides *wassel*, a quarter of a yard of roast beef for his dinner (for that monasteries did deliver their guests meat by measure), and a great black jack of strong drink. Being further asked if he remembered the dissolution of the religious houses, he said very well; and that he was between thirty and forty years of age when the order came to dissolve those in Yorkshire; and that great lamentation was made, and the country all in a tumult when the monks were turned out.

Another cause is also mentioned in which Jenkins appeared as a witness at York, in 1667, between the Vicar of Catterick and William and Peter Mawbank, in which he deposed that tithes of wool, lambs, &c, were the vicar's, and had been paid, to his knowledge, one hundred and twenty years and more.

Of the family history and private life of the venerable old man we have very little information. He was married, but what family he had we know not; two sons have been mentioned as living a few years before their father's death, " both of whom were much more infirm in memory and in body than the patriarch himself."

The multitude of great events which took place during the lifetime of this man are truly wonderful and astonishing. He lived under the rule of nine sovereigns of England—Henry VII.; Henry VIII.; Edward VI.; Mary; Elizabeth; James I.: Charles I.; Oliver Cromwell; and Charles II.; he was born when the Roman Catholic religion was established by law, he saw the dissolution of the monasteries, and the faith of the nation changed—Popery established a second time by Queen Mary—Protestantism restored by Elizabeth—the civil wars, between Charles and the Parliament begun and ended—monarchy abolished—the young Republic of England arbiter of the destinies of Europe, and the restoration of monarchy under the libertine Charles II. During his time, England was invaded by the Scots; a Scottish King was slain, and a Scottish Queen beheaded in England; a King of Spain and a King of Scotland were Kings in England; three Queens and one King were beheaded in England in his days; and fire and plague alike desolated London. His lifetime appears like that of a nation, more than an individual, so long extended and crowded with such great events.

Harrogate.   W. GRAINGE.

ANCIENT CUSTOMS IN RIPON

St. Wilfred was abbot of the monastery in Ripon in 663, and was a great benefactor to the place I understand that Ripon continues to this day to honour the memory of St. Wilfred by races which are run in his name. In addition to these races, a feast, known as Lammas Feast, was formerly held, when, on the Saturday following Lammas Day, the effigy of St. Wilfred was brought into the town with great ceremony, preceded by music. The people went out to meet the effigy, in commemoration of the return of their favourite saint and patron from exile. The following day, called St. Wilfred's Sunday, was dedicated to him. On the Monday and Tuesday there were horse races. The following is a copy of part of an advertisement from the *Newcastle Courant*, August 28th, 1725:—

To be Run For.—The usual four miles course on Ripon Common in the county of York according to articles. On Monday, the 13th of September, a purse of twenty guineas, by any horse, mare, or gelding that was no more than five years old the last grass, to be certified by the breeder; each horse to pay two guineas entrance, run three heats the usual four miles course for a heat; and carry nine stone besides saddle and bridle. On Tuesday; the 14th, the Ladies' Plate of fifteen pounds value by any horse, &c. *Women* to be the riders, each to pay one guinea entrance, three heats, and twice about the Common for a heat.

During the feast, which forty years ago continued nearly all the week, the inhabitants of Ripon enjoyed the privilege of rambling through the delightful grounds of "Studley Royal," the seat of Mrs. Laurence. On St. Wilfred's Day " the gates of this fairy region are thrown open, and all persons are allowed to wander where they please."

Forty years ago, the following ancient custom was maintained by the inhabitants of Ripon:—On Midsummer Eve, every house keeper who in the course of the year had changed his residence into a new neighbourhood spread a table before his door in the street, with bread, cheese and ale, for those who chose to resort to it. The guests, after staying a while, if the master was well-to-do, were invited to supper, and the evening was concluded with mirth and good-humour. If is said that the origin of this custom is unknown, but it is thought that it was instituted for the purpose of introducing new-comers to an early acquaintance with their neighbours, or with the more laudable design of settling differences by the meeting and mediation of friends.

A contributor to the *Gentleman's Magazine* in August, 1790, says that at Ripon, in Yorkshire, " on Easter Sunday, as soon as the service of the church is over the boys run about the streets and lay hold of every woman or girl they can and take their buckles from their shoes. This farce is continued till the next day at noon, when the females begin and return the compliment upon the men, which does not end till

Tuesday evening; nay, I was told that some years ago no traveller could pass through the town without being stopped and having his spurs taken away, unless redeemed by a little money, which is the only way to have your buckles returned."

Morley, near Leeds.   THE EDITOR.

THE HALIFAX GIBBET

HALIFAX Gibbet Law was a cruel mode of trial and execution, which existed in the forest of Hardwick (a district comprising the principal part of the parish of Halifax) till the year 1650, when the last of the victims were Abraham Wilkinson and Anthony Mitchell. "The inhabitants within the forest of Hardwicke had a certain custom," says Bentley, in his History of Halifax, "from time immemorial, that if a felon was taken within their liberty with goods, stolen out or within the liberty of the said forest, either hand-habend, back-berand, or confessand, any commodity of the value of thirteen pence halfpenny, he should, after three markets or meeting days, within the town of Halifax, next after such apprehension, and being condemned, be taken to the gibbet, and have his head cut off from his body." The felon was, however, to be publicly and deliberately tried by a sort of jury, consisting of the frith burghers within the limit. When the felon was apprehended he was immediately brought before the lord's bailiff at Halifax, who kept the common gaol of the town, had the custody of the axe, and was the legal executioner. The bailiff then issued his summons to the constables of four several townships within the liberty, to require four frith burghers within each to appear before him on a certain day to examine into the truth of the charge. At the trial the accuser and the accused were confronted before the jury, and the goods stolen were produced. If the party accused was acquitted he was instantly liberated; if condemned, he was either executed immediately, if that was the principal market day, or set in the stocks on the less meeting days with the goods on his back, if portable, or, if not, they were placed before him. The execution always took place on the great market day, in order to strike more terror into the neighbourhood. When the criminal was brought to the gibbet, which stood a little way out of the town, on the west end, the execution was performed by means of an engine, which was raised upon a platform four feet high and 13 feet square, faced on every side with stone, and ascended by a flight of steps. In the middle of this platform were placed two upright pieces of timber, 15 feet high, joined at the top by a transverse beam. Within these was a square block of wood, 4½ feet long, which moved up and down by means of grooves made for that purpose; to the lower part of this sliding block was fastened an iron axe of the weight of 7 pounds 12 ounces. The axe thus fixed was drawn up to the top by a cord and pulley. At the end of the cord was a pin, which being fixed to the block, kept it suspended till the moment of execution, when, the culprit having placed his head on the block, the pin was withdrawn, and his head was instantly severed from his body. If the offender was condemned for stealing an ox, a sheep, or a horse, the end of the rope was fastened to the beast, which being driven, pulled out the pin, and thus became the executioner. Remains of these fatal instruments may still be seen at the gaol at Halifax. The number of persons executed in Halifax under the operation of the gibbet law during little more than a century, namely, between 1541 and 1650, amounted to no less than 49. On January the 4th, 1643, two soldiers were hanged at Halifax on a gallows made near the gibbet, for deserting from the Parliament army at Halifax to the King's forces at Heptonstall. They were taken by Sir Francis Mackworth's company, and executed the same night.

Woodhouse.   F. BLACKETT.

OBSERVANCE OF SAINTS' DAYS

THE custom of observing Saints' Days at the Old Parish Church of Wakefield is continued to the present period. Any person who takes notice of the ringing of eight o'clock in the mornings at this place will easily know, if he is at all conversant with the symbolical practice, whether any day is a Saints' day or not. If it is *not* a Saints' Day, after the church clock has struck eight times for eight o'clock in the morning, ONE bell is rung for five minutes; but when the day *is* a Saints' Day, TWO bells are rung at eight o'clock that morning, so that the inhabitants of the town may by this means know, without having the trouble to look at the calendar, that that very day is a Saints' Day This means of ecclesiastically reminding the people of their religious duties to be performed at the church on particular days is certainly an excellent although a novel one. Prayers are still offered up or said in this ancient church on each and every of the Old Saints' Days, thus keeping up the olden practice or observance of All Saints' Days or Festivals in "All Sants' Church," as this old church at Wakefield is called; but there are now no gorgeous or superstitious pageants to dazzle the eyes of beholders, nor do many people reflect that this peculiar custom is a relic or continuation of one of the usages of the palmy days of monastic times.

South Ossett.   J HEWITT.

THE FIGHT AT ADWALTON MOOR

THE fight at Adwalton Moor took place on the 30th of June, 1643. If noticed at all in imperial history, it is in the briefest manner possible. Clarendon never once alludes to it in his "History of the Rebellion," and yet, for some reason or other, less important struggles of that period have received far more notice at the hands of contemporary writers. There were on both sides at least 15,000 engaged, and on no previous occasion since the commencement of the struggle between Charles and the Parliament had such large bodies of men been brought together in Yorkshire to contest for the supremacy of "God and the Cause" or "God and the King."

The vulgar pronunciation of the name of the moor is still "Atherton," as it seems to have been then, though it was also written "Adderton," and "Atherston," in various records of the event. It is about five miles from Leeds, and about the same distance from the town of Bradford. The Moor, at the present time, seems to be for the most part unenclosed, but it is about as unromantic a battle-field as any one could possibly visit. Here a clay hole, there an ugly mound of the black refuse of an old shallow coal pit; anon an ash heap and a stray donkey or two, while about its boundaries are factories, sheds, and cottages, in the most unpicturesque disorder. At the time, however, of which we write—before the era of long chimneys, large ironworks, and deep coal mines—standing on the west side of the Moor, on the ridge which forms part of the watershed of the Aire and the Calder, whichever way the beholder would turn, the eye would gaze upon as fair a prospect as could be found in the whole shire of York—a well-cultivated tract of country, interspersed with thrifty villages, snug hamlets, lonely farmsteads, and many a pleasant home of esquire and yoeman; while the population generally were a sturdy, resolute race of men, mostly well affected towards the Parliamentarian cause, and doubtless in subsequent years many a family group would, in the long winter evenings by the ruddy fire-light, listen, with " bated breath " and glistening eyes, to deeds of daring told by some survivor of Marston Moor, Naseby, Dunbar, and Worcester.

The prospects of the party of the Parliament were at this period of a gloomy nature throughout the country, but in Yorkshire they were particularly so. One event had happened in another part of the country which seemed of dire import to the success of the cause of the Parliament, but which it is highly probable that at that time of slow intelligence neither party engaged in the events of this day was aware of, and that was the death of the great Puritan leader, John Hampden. We may rest assured that if pious Joseph Lister had been apprised of this sad news he would not have failed to have made note of this additional piece of tribulation to the many which the good man records of this period; and had the Royalists been aware of it, they would not have failed to industriously circulate tidings which to them could not fail to be welcome, but which would fall heavy indeed on the minds and hearts of the adherents of the Parliament. Hampden received his death-wound on Chalgrove field, Buckinghamshire, on the 18th June, 1643, in a fierce encounter with Rupert. He lingered in great pain till the 24th of the same month, when his " noble and fearless spirit " passed away; and most likely before the battle of Adwalton the touching sight had been witnessed of the burial of the illustrious patriot in the parish church of Hampden, where " his soldiers, bare-headed, with reversed arms and muffled drums and colours, escorted his body to the grave, singing, as they marched, that lofty and melancholy psalm in which the fragility of human life is contrasted with the immutability of Him in whose sight a thousand years are but as yesterday when it is past, and as a watch in the night."

Howley Hall, near Batley, had been garrisoned for the Parliament by Sir John Savile, of Lupset, who, with a small body of musketeers, had withstood the assaults of Newcastle's forces for several days, but at last was obliged to yield to his immensely superior strength. Newcastle after this resolved to march to Bradford, where he might reasonably suppose the almost utter annihilation of the Fairfaxes—the father, Lord Ferdinando Fairfax, being in command there, aided by his son, Sir Thomas, afterwards the celebrated commander of the entire forces of the Parliament—would be effected. We can well understand, as Sir Thomas Fairfax wrote, that Bradford " was a very untenable place," and hearing of the design of Newcastle, the Fairfaxes resolved to march out to meet him. They had only about 3,000 men, in which number a small body of horse was included, and they possessed no artillery, while Newcastle's forces were in the proportion of four to one with artillery, and an immensely superior force of cavalry. Viewed from a civilian point, it seems ridiculous that Newcastle should deliberately wait on Adwalton Moor for the Fairfaxes, seeing that they had to march their small army up rising ground to meet him. But so it appears to have been, as Newcastle came from Honley on the 29th of June, and halted on the Moor the same evening, getting his artlllery into position, and otherwise arranging the order of battle.

Lord Fairfax had given the order for the march out of Bradford at four o'clock in the morning of the 30th June; but a Major-General Gifford stands suspected of treachery from his acting generally in a very indifferent manner on two or three occasions on this day, and he is blamed for so many delays in the early morning that it was eight o'clock before the little army of the Parliament was clear of the town. The fighting here, as fighting afterwards prevailed in the war, seems only to have been of a tame nature. The advanced guard, or "forlorn hope," of Lord Fairfax drove that of Newcastle, stationed on Westgate, or Whiskett Hill, into the main body of his army, and seems then to have allowed the Parliamentarians to draw up in "battalia." Sir Thomas Fairfax commanded the right wing, Major-General Gifford the left, and Lord Fairfax commanded in chief. The Parliamentarians appear to have made good use of the enclosed grounds, behind the fences of which musketeers were placed, who galled Newcastle's cavalry severely in a charge of ten or twelve troops for the purpose of dislodging Sir Thomas Fairfax from some vantage ground in a path called Warren's Lane. The Royalists were compelled to retreat with the loss of their commander, Colonel Howard. Another charge was made here, this time by thirteen or fourteen troops of the Royalists, when they were again repulsed, but with more difficulty, and their commander, Colonel Herne, was slain. "We pursued them," says Sir Thomas Fairfax, "to their guns." Gifford had also been hotly engaged on the left, and Newcastle, seeing the resolution of the Parliamentarians, particularly those under the command of Sir Thomas Fairfax, gave orders for a retreat, but Colonel Skirton or Sturton begged of Newcastle to be allowed to charge with a stand of pikes, which he did so effectively that, says Sir Thomas Fairfax, "he broke in upon our men, and (not being relieved by our reserves, which were commanded by some ill-affected officers, chiefly Major-General Gifford, who did not his part as he ought to do), our men lost ground, which the enemy seeing, pursued this advantage by bringing on fresh troops; ours being therewith discouraged, began to fly, and were soon routed. The horse also charged us again. We, not knowing what was done on the left wing, our men maintained their ground till a command came for us to retreat, having scarce any way left now to do it, the enemy being almost round about us, and our way to Bradford cut off." Eventually, however, young Fairfax retreated in good order to Halifax, and joined his father, Lord Fairfax, at Bradford, the same night.

Here, again, it seems astonishing that Newcastle, having succeeded in defeating and cutting in two the little army of the Parliament, should have apparently allowed that part commanded by Lord Fairfax to have got away to Bradford, and that under Sir Thomas to Halifax, and that they should actually unite their forces again the same night without any means being taken to prevent them. Neither Fairfax nor Cromwell would have used an army in this lumbering fashion; and it does not appear that when Newcastle fled across the seas after Marston Moor that the military councils of Charles lost either a very sagacious intellect or a very bold heart. It may be stated that Cromwell was not present at this fight, but was playing havoc generally among the Royalists in the eastern counties at the time. There appears to be some conflict of testimony as to the number of the slain. Markham, in his " Life of Lord Fairfax," states that there were 700. Mr. Scatcherd, who has been particularly painstaking in his account of the battle, makes no mention of those who were killed, further than he supposes that they were buried on the Moor; but it seems strange that no traces of the dead have ever been discovered, though there is no lack of other relics of the fight, such as iron and lead cannon balls, horse-shoes, bits, swords, pikes, &c., which have been turned up after the lapse of more than two centuries, many of which Mr. Scatcherd says he has in his own possession.

Beeston.   E. BELLHOUSE.

A REMARKABLE CENTENARIAN

THOUGH not born in Yorkshire, Mary Wright spent a great many years of her life in the county. She was grandmother to Alderman George Tatham, the present mayor of Leeds, who furnishes the following brief particulars of her career.

This remarkable woman was born in Edinburgh on the 31st December, 1755, and died in Leeds on the 14th of March, 1859, in the 104th year of her age, and had thus lived in the reigns of five Sovereigns, viz., George II., George III., George IV., William IV., and Victoria. Her parents were respectable Presbyterians named Bishop, and the writer remembers hearing from her how tea in those days was sold for its weight in silver, the good wives selecting their heaviest coin to place in the scale against it when buying their shilling's worth of tea, at a price equal to about eighty shillings per pound.

Mary Wright, when young, removed to London, involving a journey of about two weeks, over roads like the bullock tracks in the Transvaal, sleeping a few hours each night at some inn on the road, and at the end arriving worn out with fatigue. She was of a lively disposition, fond of amusements, such as singing, private theatricals, &c. One day, when passing through the street, a Quaker lady met her, laid her hand on her arm, and said, "Be thou faithful unto death, and I will give thee a crown of life." Mary Wright could not understand what this meant, not even knowing that the words were a Scripture quotation, and thought the woman insane. Wishing to amuse her young friends by representing what took place at a Quaker's meeting, she attended one, during the silence of which she was wonderfully visited by the Holy Spirit of God, convincing her of her sins, of the need of a Saviour, and that she could no longer take pleasure in things in which she had formerly delighted. She went home, and alone in her chamber, pondering over these things, and with prayer to be led aright, she felt constrained to strip her dress of all ornaments and finery, which at once she did, and burned them in the fire; ever afterwards seeing it to be her duty to observe great simplicity in all outward things. She continued her connection with the Friends, whom she joined, and eventually became "recorded" as a minister in that body,

She married John Witchell (a name now almost extinct in England, though still existing in Wales), who was then engaged in the banking house of Smith, Wright and Co., afterwards Smith, Payne and Co., but some years afterwards removed with her husband and youngest son to America, where she spent sixteen years, mostly in Pennsylvania and Ohio, encountering the hardships of a settler's life in those days, and earnest in her labours for the spread of "the truth," being instrumental in establishing several meetings of Friends, which still remain in those parts. In attending her "Yearly meetings," she several times crossed the Alleghany mountains on horseback, having at times to swim the rivers, she being kept on her saddle by the assistance of a man Friend on each side.

Shortly after her return to England her husband died, and after some years she married William Wright, of Sheffield, whom she survived, and eventually settled in Leeds, where she died.

Mary Wright was blessed with exceptionally good health, and preserved her faculties to the last. She was very independent in her feelings. She took great pleasure in helping the poor, and having but small means of her own, she employed herself in knitting purses, which she disposed of amongst her friends, so that she might be able to give of her own earnings to those who were in want. When turned one hundred years of age she knitted a silk purse for the Queen, which was graciously accepted. At this time five generations of the family were living, and were photographed together. The following members composed the group:—

1st. Mary Wright ... ... born 12 month	31	1755
2nd Her daughter, Ann Tatham ... „ 5 „	9	1780
3rd Her daughter, Emma Mennell ... „ 3 „	17	1803
4th Her son, Charles Isaac Mennell „ 4 „	2	1825
5th His daughter, Emma Louisa Mennell „ 6 „	26	1850

The last of these only survives.

Mary Wright's eyesight remained good, and during the Crimean war she took a deep, though distressed, interest in the accounts connected therewith, diligently reading the papers of the day without the aid of glasses; but soon after her sight failed, and for the last two or three years she was blind—her mental faculties remaining bright to the last. Within a fortnight of her death she preached very acceptably, with clearness and power, to the Friends at Camp-lane-court Meeting-house,

Mary Wright.
Aged 104.

She died peacefully on the 14th of March, 1859, and the heavenly, blissful expression of her features could leave no doubt on the minds of those who beheld it that she had gone to be at rest for ever with the Lord.

LONGEVITY IN KIRKBURTON

The following instances of extreme longevity are recorded in the register of the Parish Church of Kirby Burton :—

1655 —Elizabeth Clayton, widow, buried 20th February, aged 112 years and upwards.
1670.—Widow Lee, of Broome Bank Steele, buried 2nd March, aged 105 years.
1672.—Robert Fitton, buried 9th February, aged 94 years.
1708.—Ellen Booth, of Scholes, widow, buried July, supposed to be 100 years old.
1749.—Robert Ellis, of Barnside, Hepworth, buried 25th December, aged 103 years.
1800.—John Sykes, Snowgatehead in Fulstone, aged 101 years.
1812.—James Hinchcliffe, of Milshaw in Hepworth, clothier, buried May, aged 102 years.

The following list of the names of persons who had attained the age of 95 years and upwards in this district since 1813 has been copied from the Parochial Registers of Kirkburton and Holmfirth, and from the registers under the Registration Acts :—

1822.—Mary Hoyle, widow, Shepley, aged 95 years.
1827.—Grace Lee, of Riley, aged 99 years.
1833.—Joseph Smith, of Grange, Thurstonland, aged 96 years,
1850.—Michael Wortley, of Shepley, aged 97 years.
——— Mary Hellawell, of Cumberworth, aged 99 years.
1857.—George Chappell, of Paddock, Kirkburton, aged 100 years.

In addition to these, it may be stated that there are forty-one persons recorded to have attained the ages of from 90 to 94 years.

The registers of the Parish Church of Almondbury supply us also with the following in connection with this district :—

1506.—Elizabeth, the wife of John Green, of Holme, buried 8th April, aged 100 years.

In 1695 occurs the following remarkable record :—

Nicholas Grime, of Brockholes, buried 9th March, aged 96 years.
Dinah Kay, of Castle Hill, widow, buried 10th March, aged 105 years.
Maria Earnshaw, of Honley, widow, buried 11th March, aged 90 years.
Alice, widow of Daniel Dyson, of Crosland, buried 10th March, aged 63 years.

The Vicar adds—" These four burials took place at the Parish Church within the space of forty-eight hours, and their united ages amounted to 354 years."

Huddersfield. E. D. BOOTH,

WHITBY ABBEY

This famous Abbey was founded by Lady Hilda, whose death took place twelve hundred years ago, and an enquiry into the special circumstances which induced her to build the Abbey opens up an interesting chapter in ancient local and general history. This will be seen when we consider what England was when Hilda's Abbey and College first arose, a lighthouse above the ocean—waters in the seventh century—when it first shone like a Pharos over the old kingdom of Deira, which was one of the chief provinces of the kingdom of darkness.

England was, from North to South, along its whole eastern side, and far up in the Midland Counties, a thoroughly heathen country, and had been heathen for 200 years preceding, ever since the departure of the Romans. What makes this fact so striking and terrible is that during the 400 years of the Roman Dominion, nearly the whole country had been evangelised. St. Ninian, after whom one of Whitby's churches is named, was a Scottish nobleman educated in Rome, who became one of the chief evangelists of the ancient races during the Roman times. The British tribes, and their neighbours, the Irish people, had thus early received the Gospel. When the Saxons came and saw, and conquered Britain, they restored heathenism over the whole area of their conquests. It was almost as if an army of Hindoos should now land in England, vanquish the inhabitants, drive the remnant towards the West, and establish Indian idolatry on the ruins of our Christianity. We are the descendants of those Saxon heathens, and we still call our week days after the names of their impure gods and goddesses, Sun-day, Moon-day, Tuisca's day, Woden's, Thor's day, Freyga's day—a fearful memorial of the overthrow of the ancient British Christianity.

The conquered Britons retired westward, fighting all the way, into Cornwall, into Devonshire, into Wales, into Cumberland, and Westmoreland, and Lancashire ; and they took their Christianity and civilisation with them, leaving behind a vast and awful night of barbarous Saxon paganism—of paganism with its ignorance, ferocity, blood-thirstiness, drunkenness, and lust. Eastern and Midland England for 200 years, from the time of Hengist to the time of Hilda, was full of ferocious tribes, battling all along the west with the remnant of the British aborigines, and battling just as fiercely with each other. When St. Hilda was a young woman all central England, or Mercia, was held by a savage Pagan Sovereign named Penda, 80 years of age, a sort of Saxon Cetewayo, master of a powerful army, who for fifty years had made war upon his neighbours. And it was in consequence of the destruction of this terrible old Pagan warrior by King Oswy at Winwidfield, near Leeds, in 655, that Hilda was enabled in 658 to found her abbey. Penda had previously slain King Oswald in the west, and hanged his mangled body aloft at Oswald' tree, now Oswestry.

A monastery of the ancient ages is often thought of as necessarily an abode of idleness, and even of licentiousness. Such no doubt many of the religious houses at last became, and even this great Benedictine house at Whitby among the number in its latter days. Its present ruin is, according to Dr. Young, the visible punishment of the sins of its latest inmates. But in the earlier centuries a great monastery was often a stronghold of the good cause against the powers of darkness — and this mighty foundation of Hilda's was among the noblest in England. Its purpose can hardly be understood, unless we remember that in the first half of the seventh century, there was in all Europe no more awful Aceldama and "abomination of desolation" than this northern part of England. The Saxon Heathen and Pictish Highlanders, had repeatedly laid the land waste in their wars, and made its rivers flow with blood. The country was scarred with the black marks of conflagrations of farms and homesteads. Deira invaded Mercia, and old Mercian Penda invaded Deira again and again. Bernicia invaded Lancashire and North Wales, and North Wales invaded Bernicia and Deira, or Northumberland and Yorkshire. All the history of these parts that remains is the history of cruelty, wrong, and bloodshed. No power but one could save and civilise Saxon heathenism, and turn this hell of the angles into a paradise. That power was Christianity. The kings had begun to hear of what Christianity had done for other states and nations in Europe, and they were growing weary of their own wars and miseries. The monasteries which arose in that age, in the midst of the forests and open countries, were, then, strongholds of Christianity and civilization. A great monastery well placed aloft, like Cassino or Streonshall, and wisely and holily governed, was a Bethesda or Pool of Mercy with many porches. It was (1) a Temple for the *worship* of the living and eternal God, amidst the grotesque and degrading horrors of paganism, where the light of truth shone on high over the pagan pandemonium. (2) It was a *place of Education* for both sexes. The Princess Hilda, grand-niece of King Edwin of Northumbria, founded here (after the modern American fashion) a college and school for both sexes, for both monks and nuns. Many of these were persons, like Hilda, well on in life and weary of the world; some of these were young, some even almost boys and girls. Her first charge was the little Princess Elfreda, well-born on her mother's side; for there had been a succession of Christian Queens. First, Bertha, a French Princess, married Ethelbert, the King of Kent, and brought Christianity with her. Their daughter was Ethelburga, who married King Edwin in the great well-built Roman city of York, the capital of his kingdom of Deira. Their daughter was Eanfleda, who married King Oswy, still a heathen; and their child was Elfreda, who was educated as a Christian at Whitby. In three cases Christianity came with the wife to a pagan husband. Who could say how great a blessing, or how great a curse, every young woman carries with her in her marriage, according as she is a loving wife and worshipper of God, or a heathenish worldling. Thus a monastery was a *College and a School*, and often had a learned *Library*. We still possess the catalogue of good books in manuscript, which this Abbey treasured up in the 12th century, beginning with the Bible. Part of the work of the place always was to copy good books, the priceless legacies of elder times, as it is now a good work to give or to lend them. A monastery inspired by such persons as Hilda and her fellow-workers was next a great *mission centre*, whence educated men

Portrait of Lady Hilda (from a Scarce Print).

went forth on foot to evangelise the neighbouring villages and towns; and many were the cells and village churches which were set up by the godly monks from Whitby College. The noble St. Chad, or Ceadda, of Lindisfarn, was often here; and so holy and laborious a worker and walker was he, that the people in after-times fancied that a healing virtue remained in the springs and pools where he baptised the heathen Saxons whom he converted; so that the name of "St. Chad'swell," or Shadwell, is found over half of England, and has reached as far as London. For long Ceadda's central abode was at Lastringham, beyond Pickering; and afterwards, in his last days when full of years and honours, he was made the Bishop of Litchfield, the first of a series of eighty, ending with Bishop Maclagan.

3. A monastery was also a great *school of medicine*, and *place of healing*. There were stored up all manner of receipts, wise and unwise, for the medical use of plants and treatment of wounds. And thence went forth elder Sisters of Mercy, to nurse the poor people of Whitby 1200 years ago.

4. A great monastery was a fountain of *civilisation in all the useful arts*, such as agriculture and gardening. The best intelligence of the time was frequently brought to bear on the culture of a great abbey's possessions. It was also a *school of the fine arts*—of music, singing, painting, and preeminently of architecture. It was likewise a *school of poetry*, for here Cædmon sang his inspired song of the Creation, and commended to the semi-barbarous Saxons divine ideas in strains that echoed far and wide over Saxon England, and gave prophetic hints of Miltons of the future yet to come.

And (5) lastly, a great monastery was a visible monument of all the *Past Divine History of the world*, as well as a written prophecy of a better kingdom to come in the last days.

All this was in the design of the Princess Hilda, when she planted her great Abbey upon these heights; and since she was, beyond all reasonable doubt, a devoted Christian, her object was in a great measure realised. For the great church and college of Whitby became to Yorkshire, and far beyond it, a fountain of salvation. Her religion was clothed in the idiom, the ceremonial, the conceptions of her own day; and much of that external investure was no doubt the growth of ages of gradual departure from the apostolic model. But what a grand and noble woman was this, who kindled so great a light on that sublime eminence, the memory of whose noble works was powerful enough 400 years after her death, to create another race of men to rebuild the fallen in new splendour on the very site of her earlier enterprise.

Now arose the early monasteries of Canterbury, of Glastonbury, of Streonshall—to this last king Oswy assisting by the gift to Hilda of twelve manors, prompted thereto by the remorseful desires of a heart that repented itself of its previous blood-stained and violent career. Now henceforth the figure of the Princess Hilda rises on her sacred hill, towering aloft above the desolated villages of Saxon Deira, a true messenger of peace to the troubled people. Her monastery continued for 200 years to be the central light amongst this darkness; and the gleam that shone through the rounded windows of her humble early church was truly a light of life to the Saxons. Then, as you know, followed in the 9th century the complete destruction of the first modest and mostly wooden fabric by the Danish pirates, and an utter desolation of Streonshall for 200 years, indeed until after the Norman conquest. Then the Norman Percys, moved by the horrors of William the Conqueror's desolation of Yorkshire—as Hilda had been moved 400 years before by the similar horrors of the Saxon war desolations—began the re-building of the Abbey and Monastery, of which, and its subsequent additions, we can see the noble ruins to-day.

Now again 400 years followed of growing magnificence, of ceaseless worship, of holy song, devout study, of strenuous labour by

Ruins of Whitby Abbey.

twenty-five generations of the black-robed Benedictine monks among the surrounding towns and villages; and alas, of increasing superstition, increasing depravation of manners, increasing sloth and forgetfulness of God, until the crisis was reached of the Tudor reigns; when the voice of England, thundering indignantly like a northern tempest against the apostate Church, supported Henry VIII. in the dissolution and plunder of the Abbeys, then possessed of at least one-third of the cultivated land of the kingdom; and ruin fell upon Streonshall, with its precincts full of the dust of saints and kings, in the just judgment of God.

London.   EDWARD WHITE.

Edward Simpson, *alias* "Flint Jack."

FLINT JACK

"Flint Jack," whose proper name was Edward Simpson, but who was also known as "Fossil Willy," "Cockney Bill," "Bones,' "Shirtless," "Snake Billy," and the "Old Antiquarian," and who also assumed the *alias* of "Edward Jackson," as well as "John Wilson," "Jerry Taylor," &c., was a native of Sleights, two miles west of Whitby, in Yorkshire, where he was born in the year 1815. This I have in his own words, written down on the 10th of August, 1867 : " Born at Sleights, five miles west of Whitby. Now fifty-two years of age. Don't know when born."

His father was a sailor, and young Simpson was brought up as most young lads on the coast are, or rather were, brought up, partly on land and partly on the water. When fourteen years old he entered the service of Dr. Young, the historian, of Whitby—a man of varied attainments and an ardent geologist—from whom he acquired his love for geology and antiquities. He left Dr. Young, whom he constantly attended on his geological excursions, and entered the services of Dr. Ripley, also of Whitby, with whom he remained until the Doctor's death, which took place in about six years (1840). Thrown out of his situation, Jack, who had acquired a sound knowledge of and a deep love for paleontology, turned his attention to the collecting of fossils from the neighbourhood around Whitby, and disposing of them to the dealers and others at that place, and at Bridlington, Filey, Scarborough, etc. In this honest and praiseworthy manner young Simpson, who was then a young man of five or six and twenty, made a good living. He was very industrious in collecting specimens, and being particularly clever in cleaning fossils, obtained considerable employment.

In 1843, a dealer in " curiosities," in Whitby, with whom young Simpson did business in fossils, showed him a flint arrow head of barbed form, found somewhere in the neighbourhood, and asked him if he could make one like it? He said he would try, and this turned his attention from an honest to a dishonest calling. Being very *cute* and clever, and handy at anything, Edward Simpson soon set himself to his task of forming a counterfeit arrow head, and eventually succeeded so well that he manufactured them—of all conceivable and inconceivable forms —in large numbers, and palming them off as genuine antiques on experienced antiquaries as well as on amateurs, found a ready and profitable sale for his productions.

Having succeeded in making the flint arrow head, of which I have spoken, and having, after much patient labour, succeeded also in expertly striking off the flake from the nodules of flint and chipping them into form, he extended his love for counterfeiting ancient works of art by establishing for himself a small secret pot-work, where he busied himself in making so-called ancient urns. This was, it is stated, in 1844. " The first pottery he made," says Mr. Monkman, the writer to whom I have alluded, " was among the Bridlington clay. This was an *Ancient British Urn !* which he sold as a genuine one to Mr. Tyndall, asserting it to have been found somewhere in the neighbourhood. For a time the urn making business proved the best, and the second was sold to a Mr. Tysseman, of Scarborough, and a third to Dr. Murray." The new branch of trade even necessitated still more secrecy and still greater knavery, and Jack betook himself to the cliffs, where he set up an *ancient pottery* of his own. Here, after modelling the urns, he placed them beneath the shelter of an overhanging ledge of rock, out of reach of rain, but free to the winds, until dry. Then came the bakings. These were only required to be rude and partly effective, and the roots, grass, and brambles, afforded the "fire-holding," and with them he completed the manufacture of his *antiquities*. Jack, however, had found the clay cliff of Bridlington Bay too open and exposed, and he repaired for his study and his works to the well-wooded and solitary region about Stainton Dale, between Whitby and Scarborough, where he built himself a hut near Ravens' Hall, and used to spend a week at a time there engaged in the making of his spurious urns and stone implements. After a general "baking-day," he would set off either to Whitby or Scarborough, to dispose of his collections—all of which he most religiously declared had been found in (and taken by stealth from) tumuli (Jack says *toomoloo*) on the moor—his great field for his discoveries being the wild wastes between Kirby-Moorside and Stokesley, where he declares a man might pass a month without meeting another human being. Fear of detection, therefore, was reduced to a minimum—and the general knowledge of antiquities of the British period was then but small. The urns, therefore, were all sold as *genuine* ones, and were never suspected. Now (1866) he says they would be detected at once, being not only too thick in the walls, but altogether of wrong material, ornament, shape, and burning. "I often laugh," says Jack, " at the recollection of *the things* I used to sell in *those* days!"

In 1845 Jack says he began to extend his "walks" from Scarborough to Pickering. He got to know Mr. T. Kendall (a gentleman who has paid much attention to archæological matters), who showed him a collection of spurious flints which had been purchased as genuine ones from a Whitby dealer. These were of Jack's make, and on being asked for his opinion he frankly told Mr. Kendall he knew where they had come from, and set to work to show the method of manufacture, initiating his patron into the mysteries of forming "barbs," "hand celts," and "hammers." Jack declares the kindness of Mr. Kendall overcame him, and he for once resolved to speak the truth. He did it, and had no occasion for regret—he exposed the forgery, and retained a friend to whom he could look for a trifle when "hard up."

In the following year Flint Jack visited Malton with some of his forgeries, but here he found a rival in the fabrication of early pottery in the person of a barber, who had for some time followed that dishonest practice. He, however, sold some of his stone implements, and not long afterwards he found near Pickering an old tea-tray, and out of this 'valuable' he set to work to fashion a piece of armour. The first idea was a shield, but the 'boss' presented an insuperable difficulty, and this was abandoned for a Roman breast-plate, which was forthwith constructed. The thing was a remarkably clever production. Jack made it to fit himself, and after finishing it, put it on, and walked into Malton. On arrival he had ' an ancient piece of armour' for sale, found near the encampments at Cawthorne—and a purchaser was found in Mr. Pycock, who had not yet suspicion of Jack. The 'relic' is now at

Scarborough. The article fitted well to the arms and neck, and had holes for thong-lacings over the shoulders and round the waist. Jack walked into Malton, wearing the 'armour' under his coat."

One of his next exploits was the fabrication of a Roman mile stone which he carved with a queer inscription, buried in a field, dug up, and wheeled in a barrow to Scarborough, where he found a glad customer for his treasure. "At the same period he undertook the manufacture of seals, inscribed stones, etc. Of the latter he professed to have found one in the stream in the Pickering Marshes. In passing the railway gatehouse there he went to the stream to drink, and in so doing, said he noticed a dark stone at the bottom of the beck. This he took up and found it had letters on it! He was advised at the Old Malton public-house to take it to Mr. Copperthwaite, and did so, receiving a reward. The stone, which is now in the collection of Capt. Copperthwaite, of the Lodge, Malton, bore the inscription, 'IMP CONSTAN EBVR' round the Christian symbol, it was wet, dirty, and heavy, and seemed to be a curiosity. Jack being then little known, no suspicion of a forgery was entertained. In course of time this stone was submitted to Mr. Roach Smith, Mr. Newton, of the British Museum, and other antiquaries, but no conclusion could be arrived at respecting it, the form of it suggesting most, if anything, the ornate top of the shaft of a banner. But the ability of the Romans to work metal so well, made it unlikely that they should use so rude an ornament of stone for such a purpose, and that theory was rejected. The article still remained a puzzle, and is now regarded as a curiosity. Its parentage was afterwards discovered, and it is needless to say it proved to be the handiwork of Flint Jack.

"In 1846, a fatal change came over Jack's life. He continued to be the same arrant rogue, but in addition, he began to drink. 'In this year' says he, 'I took to drinking—the worst job yet. Till then I was always possessed of five pounds—I have since been in utter poverty, and frequently in great misery and want.' Jack seems to have been 'led away' at Scarborough. While there he had got introduced to the manager of one of the banks, but he says he could not 'do' him, for he bought no flints and only cared for fossils. Jack had not yet set about *forging* fossils as he afterwards found it expedient to do. While at Scarborough, however, he made and disposed of a 'flint comb.'* This article was a puzzle to most people, and the buyer submitted it to Mr. Bateman, who could not find any use for it except that it might have been the instrument by which tattooing of the body was effected! He remained at Scarborough a short period, and about the end of the year visited Bridlington, Hornsea, and Hull. At the latter place, being short of money he went to the Mechanics' Institute—he had 'always

---

* A flint "comb" is in the Council Room at the York Museum This was presented by a Whitby gentleman, and was described, and had all but been engraved. Mr. Monkman saw it in August last, and has no hesitation in pronouncing it to be one of Jack's forgeries, as is also the "fish-hook" which accompanies it.

been short of money since he took to drinking'—and sold them a large stone celt (trap) represented to have been *found* on the Yorkshire Wolds, The imposture was not detected. Hull proved a barren place, and not knowing or being able to find out any antiquaries or geologists, Jack crossed the Humber and walked to Lincoln. Here he called upon the curator of the Museum, and sold him a few flints and fossils—the flints being forgeries."

From Lincoln, Flint Jack proceeded to Newark, Grantham, Stamford, and Peterborough, and visited the Roman camp at Caistor, and the Water Newton camp, near Wansworth, in Northamptonshire. At Peterborough he was introduced to Dr. Henry Porter, and remained a month, frequently being employed to go out with the Doctor in fossiling expeditions. Jack, of course, did not for one moment forget "business," and a good anecdote is related of one of his tricks played off on the Doctor, who, being possessed of a nice piece of fossil wood which he wished to have in a portable form, desired Jack to make it into a seal (he had revealed his ability to *make things* to some extent). Jack, however, took part of the wood, and getting rid of the inner annular rings, formed a signet ring, very cleverly executed. Not content with furnishing the ring with a "head," he supplied the name INGVLFVS—his tale of this wonderful ring's history being that the relic had been found by a labouring man while employed in removing soil from the churchyard of Croyland Abbey and sold to a small dealer in Peterborough. In this person's possession it had remained for many years, until discovered by some one when looking for something else. The ring, Jack had *at once* "recognised" as that of Ingulfus, who presided over the monks of Croyland *circa* 1272!" From Peterborough he went on to Huntingdon and Cambridge, Brandon, Newmarket, Norwich, Yarmouth, Thetford, Ipswich, &c. From thence he made his way to Colchester, where he formed a connection with a Jew dealer, as little scrupulous as himself, and the two—the one as fabricator of spurious articles, and the other as vendor of them to the London dealers and others—did a very thriving trade for some time. Jack, however, having learned the marts at which the Jew disposed of the articles, thought, at length, that he might as well supply them without the "middleman's" aid, and so made his way by way of Chelmsford to London. " Forged antiquities were not so generally understood at that period, and Jack says he sold manufactured flints and celts in great variety to numerous dealers whose names we need not recite. He was, however, more particularly desirous of trading with Mr. Tennant, in the Strand, who, as the sequel will show, had a hand in the subsequent exposure of Jack's malpractices. On him he called to dispose of fossils only at first, but afterwards sold flints and other antiquities; not one of the dealers knowing them to be spurious. Jack, on being asked—Did you take them in at the British Museum? replied, 'Why, *of course* I did!' and again 'They have lots of my things—and good things they are, too.' He remained in London twelve months, manufacturing flints, chiefly, the whole time, obtaining his supplies of raw material by taking boat to the chalk cliff at Woolwich. At length the dealers (and the museums too) became overcharged with flints, and Jack feared their very plentifulness would arouse suspicions. He therefore resolved upon a return into Yorkshire, but by a different route, passing through the midland counties. He accordingly resumed his 'walks,' taking Ware, Hertford, Bedford, (where he found his first purchaser since leaving London) and Northampton, where he found three ready dupes—'here,' says Jack— 'I did best of any.' For all he made large collections of flints, and 'spiced' them with a few genuine fossils. Market Harbro' proved a barren place, but at Leicester he got to the museum and succeeded in disposing of flints and fossils. At Nottingham he found two antiquaries and duped both. Jack, by way of 'a rest from the cares and anxieties of business,' took a 'holiday,' to visit the battle ground of Willerby Field (Charles I. and Cromwell), and traced part of the great Roman fosse from Nottingham to Newark, Lincoln, and Brigg. From Nottingham he proceeded to Claycross, Chesterfield, and Sheffield, but did no trade, having no flint. He passed through Sheffield 'with great reluctance,' and procceded by Wakefield and Tadcaster to York, *en route* for Bridlington Bay." At York he made an arrangement to collect fossils and shells for the museum, and spent about a year faithfully upon this employment.

" In the summer of 1849 Jack set off on a fossiling expedition to the north—taking no flints with him. He walked to Staithes, Guisbro', Redcar, Stockton, and Hartlepool, and confined his attention to the selection of fossils from the magnesian limestone—fossil fish and plants. Thence he went to Darlington and Richmond, and at the latter place got to know Mr. Wood, the geologist of the mountain limestone country, and remained there all the winter collecting and cleaning fossils. In the new year of 1850 he started for Barnard-Castle, Kirkby-Stephen, Kendal, Ambleside, Keswick, Cockermouth, Whitehaven, Workington, Maryport, and Carlisle—the whole of these walks being *nil*. Thence he went to Wigton, Austin-Moor, Haltwhistle, and Hexham, where he halted for the purpose of visiting Hadrian's wall. He was much pleased with this locality, and noticed several Roman votive altars in the old walls, frequently in the walls of stables, and piggeries. Jack eventually reached Newcastle, where he had no difficulty in selling out his accumulation of fossils at the Museum. Jack's northern tour, up to this period, had been of a faultless complexion, but he, unfortunately, walked to North Shields, and examined the shingle on the beach and 'found some flint.' Here was a temptation not to be withstood, and Jack set to work on the spot to make forged celts, and with a spurious collection he went to Durham and there lapsed into his old trade, selling a few as genuine (with a plausible history attached) to private individuals who ' took an interest in *antiquities*.' From Durham he made for Northallerton, and at Broughton, a village four miles distant, he managed to 'do' a gentleman by selling him flints. By way of Thirsk, Easingwold, Helmsley, Kirby, and Pickering, he reached Scarbrough, the district yielding him but little profit. Afterwards, Jack having replenished his stock, made two separate tours into Westmoreland with his fossils and forged flints, which he sold to a banker at Kendal, to a barber at Ambleside, to Flintoff's Museum at Keswick, and also to a private gentleman there. While here he took to wood carving, and to the formation of seals, rings, and beads, in coal and amber, and sold these readily at the Lakes."

In the next season, he went to Ireland by way of York, Leeds, Manchester, and Liverpool, selling his counterfeits at each place on his route. His Irish tour was a very profitable one, and after a time he recrossed the channel, and came back to his original haunt at Bridlington. In 1852, he was employed in collecting fossils for some gentlemen of Scarbro' and Whitby, and then again set out for London, staying a long time on his way, at Bottesford, collecting and disposing of fossils from the lias there.

After visiting Scotland and other places, Jack in 1859 made a very profitable journey into Cumberland, going by Houghton-le-Spring, Durham, Barnard Castle, and Brough, to Lancaster, and across the sands of Morecambe Bay to Ulverstone, Bootle, and Ravenglass—then Whitehaven. He walked from Whitehaven to Carlisle in one day, and thence to Longtown, Haltwhistle, Hexham, Newcastle, Durham, Darlington, Richmond, Leyburn. Kettlewell, Harrogate, and Leeds. This was entirely a flint selling journey—occasionally he made an urn, or forged a fossil, and carried them on the road till a customer turned up. From Leeds he went to Selby and Hull, and took the boat to Grimsby, going by Louth to Boston, Spalding, and Lynn, selling flints and lias fossils all the way.

In 1861, Flint Jack again visited London, and was again employed by Mr. Tennant, but the fact of his flints being spurious having got pretty well, by this time, bruited about, that gentleman taxed him with their manufacture (which it is but fair to Jack to say he had on more than one occasion openly acknowledged), to which soft impeachment he was not slow to plead guilty. Mr. Tennant proposed to introduce him to meetings of the Geological Society and other societies, if he would exhibit, publicly, his method of forming flint and stone implements, for which of course he was to be recompensed. Accordingly, on the 6th of January, 1862, " a considerable gathering of geologists and their friends took place at the rooms in Cavendish Square, in which at that time the meetings of the Geologists' Association were held, under the presidency of Professor Tennant. Two popular subjects were announced for the evening's consideration; the one being on 'Lime and Lime-stones,' by the President; the other, 'On the ancient Flint Implements of Yorkshire, and the Modern Fabrication of similar specimens,' by the Rev. Thomas Wiltshire, the Vice-President. These announcements attracted a full attendance of members, and of their wives and daughters. The ladies rapidly filled the upper portion of the lecture-room nearest the platform ; but courteously left the foremost row of seats to be occupied by the friends of the President and the Committee. It soon became evident that it was to be a crowded meeting, and as the back seats gradually filled, many a wistful glance was cast at these reserved seats ; yet, by common consent they were left vacant. Presently, however, an individual made his way through the crowd whose strange appearance drew all eyes toward him, and whose effrontery in advancing to the foremost seats, and coolly sitting down in one of them, was greeted by a suppressed titter on the part of the ladies. He was a weather-beaten man of about forty-five years of age, and he came in dirty tattered clothes, and heavy navvy's boots, to take precedence of the whole assemblage; it was natural, therefore, that the time spent in waiting for the President's appearance should be occupied in taking an inventory of his curious costume and effects. He wore a dark cloth coat, hanging in not unpicturesque rags about the elbows ; it was buttoned over a cotton shirt which might once have been white, but which had degenerated to a yellow brown. About his neck was a fragment of a blue cotton handkerchief ; his skin was of a gipsy brown, his hair hung in lank black locks about a forehead and face that were not altogether unprepossessing, except for the furtive and cunning glances which he occasionally cast around him from eyes that did not correspond with each other in size and expression. His corduroys, which were in a sorry condition, had been turned up ; and their owner had evidently travelled through heavy clay, the dried remains of which bedaubed his boots. Altogether he was a puzzling object to the ladies ; he had not the robust health or the cleanliness of a railway navvy ; he differed from all known species of a London working man ; he could scarcely be an ordinary beggar 'on the tramp,' for by what means could such an individual have gained admittance to a lecture-room in Cavendish-square ? Yet this last character was the one best represented by the general appearance of the man, who carried an old greasy hat in one hand, and in the other a small bundle tied up in a dingy red cotton handkerchief. The most amusing part was the comfortable assurance with which he took his seat, unchallenged by any of the officials, and the way in which he made himself at home by depositing on the floor, on one side his hat, on the other side his little red bundle, and then set to work to study the diagrams and specimens which were displayed on the platform.

"At length the President, Vice-president, and Committee entered the room, and the business of the evening commenced. Many glances were cast at the stranger by the members of the Committee, but no one seemed astonished or annoyed at his presence ; and, in fact, he was allowed to retain the prominent position which he had chosen for himself. He listened attentively to the President's lecture, and to the discussion which followed ; but his countenance betrayed a keener interest when the second paper of the evening, that on Yorkshire Flint Implements, was read. And here the mystery of the stranger was suddenly revealed, for in the course of his remarks on the clever fabrications of modern times, by which these ancient flint instruments were successfully copied, the Vice-president stated that, through the efforts of Professor Tennant, a person was in attendance who, with the aid of only a small piece of iron rod, bent at the end, would, with remarkable dexterity, produce almost any form of flint weapon desired. He then desired the stranger to mount the platform, and the man, taking up his hat and bundle, seated himself in a conspicuous position, and prepared to exhibit his skill. He undid the knots of his red handkerchief, which proved to be full of fragments of flint. He turned them over, and selected a small piece, which he held sometimes on his knee, sometimes in the palm of his hand, and gave it a few careless blows with what looked like a crooked nail. In a few minutes he had produced a small arrow-head, which he handed to a gentleman near, and went on fabricating another with a facility and rapidity which proved long practice. Soon a crowd had collected round the forger, while his fragments of flint were fast converted into different varieties of arrow-heads, and exchanged for sixpences among the audience. This was the first appearance before the public, in London, of the celebrated " Flint Jack.' "

In 1863, Flint Jack was again at Salisbury, but here, says my late friend Mr. Stevens, the then honorary curator of the museum, " his career in deception was very short," as he (Mr. S.) at once found out that the flints he offered for sale were forgeries. Mr. Stevens here, at his own expense, had Jack's portrait taken in photography by Mr. Treble, from which the accompanying engraving is made. Mr. Stevens here gave him employment by ordering him to make him a complete set of flints for exhibition, and these are now placed in a frame along with the photograph and a brief memoir of Flint Jack, in the Museum at Salisbury, as a " caution to the unwary."

After poor " Flint Jack', lost his occupation through being induced to make public confession and exhibition of his forgeries of antique flint implements and the like, he passed a nomadic life as a miserable lost wanderer, often on the point of actual starvation, and always in abject poverty. He tried hard, poor fellow, to make a living by collecting, during his wanderings, such fossils and other " curiosities" as came in his way, and parting with them for a few pence here and there, and occasionally making here and there an imitation flint implement, or a stone hammer or two, and selling them to those who cared to possess them—and he was often reduced to the necessity of actual begging. One of his failings was intemperance, and in his weak state wanting food, the slightest indulgence took effect upon him. Thus in the month of January, 1867, in a time of very severe weather, while endeavouring to make his way to London, he got as far as Bedford, when he called, in a pitiable and starving condition, upon some gentlemen who gave him timely help in food and clothes, as well as means to help him on to the metropolis. Instead of proceeding thither, however, his love of drink overcame him, and, while in that state, he committed two petty robberies—the one of a barometer, the other of a clock—for which he was taken into custody, and, happily, as providing a home for him, was sentenced to one year's imprisonment in Bedford gaol.

While there incarcerated, I took occasion to communicate with the then governor of the gaol, Mr. Roberts, and through him with the wretched man himself. The result was, that through an "appeal" which I made, I was fortunate enough to obtain a small fund which I placed in the hands of the governor of Bedford gaol, so that on his release in the following March, some clothes were provided for him, a railway ticket to the destination (Cambridge) he desired to go to, and a sum of money given him to make a fresh start, the remainder being sent to him, a pound at a time, so long as it lasted, and until he obtained other means of obtaining an honest livelihood.

The poor fellow is now dead, but the memory of his good qualities—for he was not devoid of them—and of his undoubted cleverness still lives, and is cherished by no one who knew him more highly than myself. He deserved a better fate, and had he been properly taken in hand in earlier years, would have become a valuable and highly useful member of society.

The Hollies, Duffield, Derby.   LLEWELLYNN JEWITT, F.S.A.

BOLLING HALL

BRADFORD is not so rich in historic relics and associations as some other towns in Yorkshire that might be named, and the stranger on the look out for antiquities would fail to meet with the quaint old gables, and the overhanging houses, with their mullioned and diamond-paned windows, that carry one back at a glance to the fifteenth and sixteenth centuries. But it possesses, nevertheless, one of the finest old baronial mansions that can be found in the West-Riding — a relic "familiar with forgotten years, and with the history of the olden time" written upon its very walls.

Bolling Hall occupies a commanding position, and a glance from this eminence is sufficient to take in a fine view of its general surroundings. In the valley below lies the dingy town, for Bradford still looks dingy from its outskirts, notwithstanding the recent improvements in the way of smoke consumption, and it requires a fair stretch of the imagination to picture it as it was in the far off time when but a mere village, composed of rudely thatched cottages, interspersed by the burgage-houses, with their crofts and foldsteads, which then served as the mansions of the "better sort."

To form a fair conception of the age of Bolling Hall, we must glance across the page of history far beyond the days when John Bunyan was a prisoner in Bedford gaol, and even beyond the Wars of the Roses, before we approach that remote period (the 14th century) when William de Bolling, lord of the manor of Bolling, gave certain "common of pasture" pertaining to the same manor, to Kirkstall Abbey, and twelve acres of land in Bolling, (in modern times called Bowling) to the Hospital of St. Peter, York, in " pure alms." Going further back still, we are told of a certain Sindi, who was the owner of Bolling, for is it not recorded in the Doomsday Book, that "In Bollinc Sindi hath four carucates of land," and that " Illbert (de Lacy) has it and it is waste; value in King Edward's (the Confessor) time, five shillings?"

The Bollings appear to have been a thriving and influential family in their day and generation. A Robert de Bolling, who died in the reign of Henry III. was probably the next owner of the estate after Sindi, and may have been a descendant of his, seeing that "the posterity of these Saxons frequently assumed local names from the places of their residence." A long run of good fortune seems to have followed the Bollings down to the adventurous reign of Edward IV., when the unfortunate struggles for supremacy between the houses of York and Lancaster threw the whole country into war. Lord Clifford, of Skipton Castle, espoused the cause of the Lancastrians, and carried things with a high hand among the Yorkshire gentry who hardly dared do other than enrol themselves under his banner. The famous battle of Towton, was fought on Palm Sunday, March 29th, 1461 and resulted in the defeat of the Lancastrians, and the slaughter of 36,000 men. Among the defeated ones, perhaps none suffered more than did Robert de Bolling (the third of that name.) He was attainted for high treason against the King, and in an Act of Resumption of forfeited estates made in 1468 it was specially provided that the Act " should not be to the prejudice of Thomas Radclyff, Esquire, of the *grant to him* made by letters patent *of the Manor of Bolling.*

Nothing is recorded to show what became of the attainted Robert during the time that he was kept out of his estate by Radclyff, and it must be left to conjecture as to how he and his wife, and ten children, obtained a "lyvelode" while in so sorry a plight. However, he petitioned the King in pitiful terms to restore him to his estate, assuring his " Highness that he was never against him, in any feld or journey, except on Palm Sunday . . . whereto he was dryven, not of his own proper wille, ne of malice toward youre Grace, but oonly by compulsion, and by the most drad proclamations of John then Lord Clyfford, under whose daunger and distresse the lyvelode of your suppliant lay."

Whatever may have been the effect upon the King of this appeal, it is satisfactory to know that Robert de Bolling eventually recovered his forfeited estates, and that he made his will, at Bolling Hall, in which he directed that his body should be buried before the altar in Bradford Church.

Of the Bollings who succeeded the unfortunate Robert there are none who call for special notice till we come to Tristram, at whose death, without male issue, the line of the Bollings of Bolling (reaching over nearly four hundred years) became extinct. Tristram had an only daughter, named Rosamond, who married Sir Richard Tempest, of Bracewell, a man of some note in his day. Rosamond appears to have

Bolling Hall.

made him a worthy partner and to have fully sustained her position as the wife of a great man, for Tempest was High Sheriff of Yorkshire, and at the Field of Flodden had held a principal command under the Earl of Surrey. She bore him nine children, all of whom grew up and married with some of the best families of the county. The fifth son, Henry, married Ellinor, daughter of Christopher Mirfield, of Tong Hall, by which union Henry acquired the Tong estate, and become the founder of the Tempests of Tong.

There was a long succession of Richard Tempests at Bolling Hall, the last of whom, however, seems to have been no credit to the family. He is described as "a weak imprudent man;" but it was his misfortune to live in disturbed times. The Civil Wars of the time of Charles I. brought ruin and disaster to many a noble family. Tempest was a gay cavalier, and for espousing the cause of the King was entrusted with the command of a regiment of horse. But he was on the losing side, and on the overthrow of the royal cause was fain to escape the forfeiture of his estates by the payment of a sum little short of two thousand pounds—a large amount at that day.

Sir Richard was his own greatest enemy. He was a reckless gamester, and tradition kindly steps in to tell us how it came to pass that he was the last of the long line of Tempests of Bolling Hall. While engaged in a game of "put," in which he had a run of bad luck, he foolishly staked the hall and estate, and as the cards were being dealt, exclaimed—

> "Now ace, deuce, and tray,
> Or farewell Bolling Hall, for ever and aye."

And thus, says tradition, the old hall that had been the home of his ancestry for a century and a half, was hopelessly lost. The last chapter in the mad career of this reckless man, was his death (1657) in the confines of the King's Bench prison, while in custody as a prisoner for debt.

The story of the Bolling Hall Ghost is a thrice told tale. The narrative runs that while the Earl of Newcastle was sleeping in one of the rooms of the Hall on the eve of the day that was to witness the destruction of Bradford, a lady in white came into the room, pulled the clothes off the Earl's bed several times, and cried out with a lamentable voice, "Pity poor Bradford." That then he sent out his orders that neither man, woman, or child should be killed in the town, and that upon hearing this good news, the apparition which had so disturbed the noble lord, quietly took its departure. Several versions have been given of this mysterious visitation, and not a few have tried to account for it, or to "explain it away." For ourselves we prefer to take the legend, for such it is, simply on its merits, and without venturing any apology for it whatever. It is enough to know that the earl gave final orders that the people should be spared, and that he speedily withdrew his troops from the town, to the no small joy and relief of many who were quaking with fear, believing that verily they were in the jaws of death.

From the Tempests, Bolling Hall passed to the Saviles of Thornhill, about the middle of the seventeenth century.

Afterwards Francis Lindley, son of William Lindley, a merchant of Hull, came into possession of the manor by purchase; and a descendant of his, Francis Lindley Wood, disposed of the manor and estate in 1816, to Messrs. John Sturges, Thomas Mason, and J. G. Paley, for £20,000, having previously disposed of the minerals to the proprietors of the Bowling Ironworks for a still larger sum.

By the kind permission of Mr. James H. Tankard, J.P., the present tenant, the writer of this sketch, visited the hall a short time ago. In the interior a special feature of interest was the large central hall with its fine front window looking on to the lawn, its quaint wooden gallery, its collection of relics—battle-axes, spears, cross-bows, and other implements of warfare; its portraits of warriors clad in heavy armour, ladies dressed in Elizabethan costume, and feudal lords, gay cavaliers, and titled gentry of more modern times. We saw the ghostly bedroom but not the ghost. It is a small apartment with just one small window looking to the South. In it is hung the portrait of Rosamond, the connecting link between the Bollings and the Tempests.

For fully five hundred years the storm beaten walls of Bolling Hall have withstood the ravages of time. Built in a style that may be best described as half castle and half mansion, with heavy walls composed of rough unsquared stones, it has come down to our own day in a condition such as few of the monuments of feudal times in Yorkshire can now boast.

West Bowling, Bradford. WILLIAM SCRUTON.

ILLUSTRATIONS OF FOLK LORE

AMONGST old Yorkshire men, and women too, there is no lack of folk-lore. Before looking at a few examples, it is worth while seeing what the derivation of this expressive term "Folk-lore" is. *Folc*, the folk *i.e.*, the common folk, or people, and *Laer*, *Lora*, learning, doctrine, precept, law; and thus from two good old English words a compound term is formed, *Folc-lare*. The word was first used in its present sense, I believe, by the editor of *Notes and Queries* (the serial), who found it to be a suitable and comprehensive title for the varied and miscellaneous gatherings of local traditions, superstitions, and proverbs, which have been handed down from generation to generation. Charms and spells are common, but not peculiar, to boyhood's warts in Yorkshire. They have been and are still used in giving relief to diseases and ailments; warts, toothache, ague, &c., are all provided for. A young lady of our acquaintance informs us that her uncle, who was a farmer at a small village just outside Leeds, cured her of a stubborn wart on one of her hands by means of a black snail. He rubbed the wart with the under side of the snail, and afterwards transfixed the poor little thing on a thorn of the garden hedge. Strange as it may seem, the wart soon disappeared. An old woman in the same village acquired great notoriety as a successful remover of warts. Her method was to tie a piece of thread round the wart, and, after tying a knot, this thread was slipped off and taken possession of by the old lady, who would never tell what she did with it. Another mode is to cut as many notches in a piece of stick as you have warts. The stick is then buried, and as it decays the warts vanish.

The following incident occurred in the neighbourhood of Leeds:—
The bishop, at a confirmation held in a village church, some two or three years ago, particularly noticed a poor, decrepit, old woman, of

whom he had a strong recollection that he had seen before. On inquiry he found that this was the third time the old lady had presented herself for confirmation. After the ceremony was over he determined to ask the old woman her reason for this repetition, and was astonished to receive the answer that she thought the "laying on of hands" did her rheumatics good.

Omens and predictions of future events are still in use amongst the Yorkshire villagers. Should you spill salt, or carelessly cross the knives, they are omens of evil in many a household. Should you, with mistaken courtesy, offer to help another with salt, you are immediately prevented, and the proverb, "Help me to salt, help me to sorrow," is repeated. A bright spark in the wick of the candle is a forerunner of the letter you are sure to receive the next day. A flake of soot hanging to the firegrate is called a "stranger," if on the top bar it is a man, if on the second bar a woman, who is the strange visitor. The soot flake is watched, and, if it falls on the hearth, "A stranger on the floor is a beggar at your door"; if it falls into the fire, "A stranger in the fire is one whom you desire." Another way is to clap the hands close to the fire, endeavouring to make the flake fall, repeating at the time the names of the days of the week, and when the soot falls the day is thus discovered on which the visitor may be expected.

If a loud, mysterious tap is heard, as of a bullet falling on a table, or three successive strokes upon the chamber floor or any of the doors, the hearer is either doomed soon to die or to hear of the death of a near and dear friend. A cinder thrown out of the fire is eagerly examined, and, if it is long and hollow, is called a coffin; if it is round it is said to be a purse. Many spit on the money they receive in payment for the articles they sell, and others carry a crooked sixpence, or a coin with a hole through it, "for luck." If you have money in your pocket the first time that you hear the cuckoo you will never be without all the year. A little lad who wears a new suit of clothes for the first time generally visits the neighbours' houses to show his finery and receive from them lucky pennies to put in his pockets. A custom akin to this is in vogue on the Borders, where no one will put on a new coat without first placing some money in the right-hand pocket. This ensures the pocket being always full, but if the unlucky wight should inadvertently put the cash in the left-hand pocket, he will never have any money so long as he wears the coat. A knife is accounted an unlucky present, as it is said to sever friendship or love. To see a strange pigeon alight upon the roof is to see an omen of sickness which is about to fall upon one of the family. When the pigeons congregate upon the ridge of the roof, and the horses in the field stand with their backs towards the hedge, it is a certain sign of rain. It is said to be the same if the cat sits on the hearth with her back to the fire. Cats have a wonderful reputation; they are said to be weather wise, to be able to see better in the dark than in daylight, to have nine lives, and are said to "draw your health away" if they are allowed to sleep with you. To have a black cat is considered a source of good luck to all the occupants of the house where it is kept. If you turn your money over in your pocket when you first see the new moon you will always have plenty there. The new moon is often anxiously watched for by the farmers, and, if it "stands upright," is said to betoken fair weather; but if, on the contrary, it leans backward, it is said to hold water, and bad weather is predicted.

Brand, on the authority of Aubrey, states that, amongst the vulgar in Yorkshire, it was believed, "and perhaps is in part still," that, after a person's death, the soul went over Whinney Moor (Winmoor, near Leeds?); and till about 1624, at the funeral, a woman came (like a Præfica) and sung the following song:—

> This ean night, this ean night,
>   Every night and awle;
> Fire and fleet (water) and candle light,
>   And Christ receive thy sawle.
>
> When thou from hence doest pass away,
>   Every night and awle,
> To Whinny-Moor (silly poor) thou comest at last,
>   And Christ receive thy sawle.
>
> If ever thou gave hosen or shoon (shoes),
>   Every night and awle,
> Sit thee down and put them on,
>   And Christ receive thy sawle.
>
> But if hosen and shoon thou never gave naen,
>   Every night and awle,
> The whinnes shall prick thee to the bare-beane,
>   And Christ receive thy sawle.
>
> From Whinny-Moor that thou mayest pass,
>   Every night and awle,
> To Brig of Dread thou comest at last,
>   And Christ receive thy sawle.
>
> From Brig of Dread, na brader than a thread,
>   Every night and awle,
> To purgatory fire thou com'st at last,
>   And Christ receive thy sawle.
>
> If ever thou give either milke or drink,
>   Every night and awle,
> The fire shall never make thee shrink,
>   And Christ receive thy sawle.
>
> But if milke nor drinke thou never gave naen,
>   Every night and awle,
> The fire shall burn thee to the bare beane,
>   And Christ receive thy sawle.

If the bed on which a dying person is laid contains pigeons' feathers, it is said to deter the death of the sufferer, and so cause them to die hard. So strong is this superstition that cases are known where the dying man has been carried on to a flock bed to enable him to die peacefully. In Leeds it is still usual in many households to place a plate of salt on the stomach of a corpse immediately after death. Salt is an emblem of eternity and immortality, and is not liable to corruption itself, and it preserves other substances from decay, so that its use in the above case is of emblematical import.

In this part of the county a superstition used to obtain that if any one troubled with warts would rub them with cinders, wrap the cinders up in a rag, throw them over head without looking behind, they would lose the warts; and any one finding the cinders would, unfortunately, become troubled with the warts. Now, if ever any one tested this seemingly ridiculous cure, and lost the warts, it would certainly perpetuate the tradition. We are apt in these enlightened days to discard such stories; we credit them to the ignorance of the people. We are unable, however, to account for some of these stories, which certainly had a beginning, whether founded upon fact or fiction.

Worcester.   SAMUEL SMITH.

NIDDERDALE

THOSE who think with George Eliot that Leisure is dead—gone with the stage coaches and the spinning jenny, and with the old chapmen who brought bargains to the door on sunny afternoons, will hardly believe, perhaps, that we possess here in Yorkshire, a picturesque bit of England of the Crusades, where the shrill whistle of the steam-engine has never yet been heard, where a newspaper is never seen except upon the breakfast table of the vicar, and where the peasantry still talk at their own firesides in a dialect which is older than the towers of Beverley or the choir of York. There is no more romantic spot in England than Nidderdale. Yet how many people, even in Yorkshire, know anything of Nidderdale, and out of Yorkshire, of course, Nidderdale is a mere *terra incognita*. The most careless must find something to interest him in a dale which has retained to this day the primitive usages of our early ancestors, where the people speak a language which contains a large admixture of Old Norsk, Gaelic, Welsh, Danish, and Gothic words; a dale which was startled to its depths, just about the time when the steam-engine was startling the greater world, by the appearance within it of the first vehicle on wheels which had ever traversed its solitudes. There is good reason to suppose that the Nidderdale of to-day is the most perfect survival we have of England as it was when William rose and Harold fell. The dale covers an area of something like eighty square miles, lying in the basin of the Nidd above Hampsthwaite. The northern and more elevated portion of the dale is pregnant with interest for the antiquary, the philologist, and the lover of stretches of wild moorland. The southerly portion, save for the magnificent Brimham Rocks, is comparatively tame.

The visitor to the valley of the Nidd, between Otley and Pateley Bridge, is, to all intents and purposes, in another world. The millstone grit rises up on each side of the valley in lines of fine escarpment, terrace above terrace, in a manner peculiar to the valleys of the Pennine Chain. Europe has nothing else like it. There is nothing so curious either in Norway or Switzerland. The margins of the terraces are frequently marked by lines of wood, but the terraces and slopes themselves are grazing land. Nidderdale is almost entirely given up to grazing, and is, in fact, one great sheep farm. It has its own breed of sheep, which is formed by the crossing of Scotch ewes and Leicester tups or mugs. Until half a century ago the dale had also its own breed of cattle—the prototypes of the famous Dun Cow of the inn signs. This breed is now practically extinct in England, but is common enough in the Norwegian dales. Its place has been taken by the famous Yorkshire shorthorns, of which Nidderdale was the nursery. The wild and half-cultivated land in this primitive dale—such of it as is not still a mere stretch of brown and purple moorland—was once under the plough; but Nidderdale has shared the fate of the Scotch glens, and sheep and cattle graze where corn once grew. The formation of sheep "gaits" and cattle runs has depopulated the dale very rapidly of late years. Numbers of small farms have been thrown into one, and the farm hands thus thrown out of employment have found their way into Leeds and Bradford to complicate the struggle for subsistence which is already sufficiently difficult in those dense populations. The increase of grazing has been the ruin of the agriculture of Nidderdale. The farmsteads of what were once arable farms are deserted and ruinous, the fences are gapped and broken, and sheep have completely usurped what was once a fairly-well populated dale. So silent and deserted are now some parts of Nidderdale that if one of its olden inhabitants could revisit the scene of his earthly pilgrimage he would inevitably believe that the tide of war had rolled over the dale and left this desolation in its wake.

"In passing up the valley from Pateley Bridge, by one of the pleasantest of roads, in the summer season, New Bridge is to be seen on the right, a narrow single arch, crossing the river into the adjoining township of Fountain's Earth. It is of considerable antiquity, only intended for foot passengers, or pack horses, and, in conjunction with a few old oaks, on the southern side, has a pretty pictorial appearance and is withal a pleasing memento of a past age.

Gouthwaite Hall is situate in an indentation of the valley close to the foot of the hills, at the opening of a woody glen called Burn Gill, Overshadowed by lofty groves of ash and sycamore, this antique mansion is a highly interesting feature in the landscape. It was probably built on an old monastic site by Sir John Yorke, early in the seventeenth century, and was the occasional residence of that family for one hundred and fifty years. The general plan is an oblong square, with projecting portions, north and south; the principal front is to the southward, and consists of two parts, one presenting the side wall, and the other the gable to the observer. The entrance, low and plain, is very singularly placed near the south-east corner. The whole building is of stone, and the covering of thick slates, grey with age and covered with lichens. The easterly part of the interior possesses, at the present time, most of the original features. The kitchen yet preserves the old chimney, four yards wide, up which the blazing fire of logs has roared merrily in days of yore. The staircase has undergone but slight modifications, being upwards of six feet wide, with the steps of solid oak two inches in thickness. In some one of the many rooms of this house, Eugene Aram taught a school, having under his care some youths who were afterwards distinguished in the world."*

Gouthwaite Hall.

There still exist among the sparse and scattered dwellers in Nidderdale many old world manners and customs, and a large share of old time forms of speech. The dale sheep are still sheared upon the ancient "sheep-cratch,"—a frame, shaped like a broad ladder, and erected horizontally, one end being supported upon two legs, and the other curving down until the ends rest upon the ground. In the upper part of the country the cheese is still pressed by the primitive arrangement of a heavy stone, worked by a wooden lever; and it is not so long ago that the Nidderdale farmers gave up making their own rush candles. To enter a Nidderdale interior, until very lately, was, at night time, very much like entering the witches' cavern in *Macbeth* when the magic cauldron was boiling. There was no light save that given by the peat

---

*Grainge's Nidderdale.

flame, and in the gloom "ayont the ingle" sat the "goodman." Mr. Lucas, the author of "Studies in Nidderdale," in one of these old farm-houses saw "two venerable dames, bent nearly double with age, and resting with both hands upon high sticks with crooked handles. On their heads they wore high caps, having an enormous frill over the top of the head and rising behind in a very tall rounded peak,"—for all the world like the traditional witches of the picture story-books. The Celt, the Roman, and the Dane have each left footprints in Nidderdale; and that there was formerly a considerable Gaelic population does not admit of doubt. The bold and rugged scenery of the dale is the fit surrounding of a people so primitive in their speech, so conservative in their habits, and so retentive of ancient customs. There is something inexpressibly grand in the stupendous size and the unequalled beauty of a scar, such as are to be found in plenty in Nidderdale. There is an attraction about a scar which an ordinary mass of rock lacks. In this secluded dale almost everything is full of peculiar interest. Over these few square miles of country we can trace the growth of the domestic history of England. Here are—or very recently were—the peat fires and the cozy ingle-nooks of our Saxon forbears; here sheep are still counted in the ancient Cymric dialect of the Pennine Chain; here are kept up Yule-tide customs which were old when Alfred reigned; and here we have a genuine bit, and mayhap the last survival, of genuine old English habits and customs. Nidderdale is, indeed, unique, and it says much for Yorkshire that, so close to teeming populations, she should have kept sacred this most enchanting of British dales.

POPULAR RHYMES AND PROVERBS

HE following Yorkshire Proverbs are taken from a "Collection of English Proverbs, with Annotations, by John Ray, M.A., and Fellow of the Royal Society," (1678.) This learned and ingenious author published two editions of the "Proverbs," and since his death several other editions have appeared. For information respecting the Yorkshire Proverbs, Ray acknowledges his indebtedness to Francis Jessop, Esq , of Broomhall in Sheffield, Francis Brokesby, of Rowley, East Riding, and others. In the following list, the quaint and homely comments of Ray as to the meaning of the proverbs will be found to be of an interesting character. His definition of a "proverb" was, that it consists of a short sentence or phrase in common use, containing some trope, figure, homonymy, rhyme, or other novity of expression.

"From Hell, Hull, and Halifax, good Lord deliver us."

"This is a part of the beggars' and vagrants' litany. Of these three frightful things unto them, it is to be feared that they least fear the first, conceiving it the furthest from them. Hull is terrible to them as a town of good government, where beggars meet with punitive charity, and it is to be feared, are oftener corrected than amended. Halifax is formidable to them for the law thereof; whereby thieves taken in the very act of stealing cloth are instantly beheaded by an engine, without any further legal proceedings. Doubtless the coincidence of the initial letters of these three words helped much the setting on foot this proverb."

"A Scarborough Warning."

"That is none at all but a sudden surprise; when a mischief is felt before it is suspected. This proverb is but of a hundred and four years' standing, taking its original from Thomas Stafford, who, in the reign of

Queen Mary, A.D. 1557, with a small company, seized on Scarborough Castle (utterly destitute of provision for resistance), before the townsmen had the least notice of his approach. However, within six days, by the industry of the 'Earl of Westmoreland, he was taken, brought to London, and beheaded."

"As true steel as Rippon rowels,"

"It is said of trusty persons, men of mettle, faithful in their employments. Rippon in this county is a town famous for the best spurs of England, whose rowels may be enforced to strike through a shilling, and will break sooner than bow."

"A Yorkshire Way-bit."

"That is an over-plus not accounted for in the reckoning, which sometimes proves as much as all the rest. Ask a country-man how many miles it is to such a town, and he will return commonly, so many miles and a way-bit, which way-bit is enough to make the weary traveller surfet of the length thereof. But it is not *way-bit*, though generally so pronounced; but wee-bit, a pure Yorkshirism, which is a small bit in the Northern language. A Highlander would say, a mile and a *bittock*, which means about two miles."

"When Sheffield Park is plowed and sown,
Then little England hold thine own."

Might this proverb have some connection with the village called Wales, in the neighbourhood of Sheffield? Pembrokeshire was formerly called "Little England beyond Wales." See Mr. Greenwell's Notes on Wales, in "Place-Names," vol. I., p. 211.

"Winkabank and Temple Brough
Will buy all England through and through."

"Winkabank is a wood upon a hill near Sheffield, where there are some remainders of an old Camp. Temple Brough stands between the Rother and the Don, about a quarter of a mile from the place where these two rivers meet. It is a square plot of ground encompassed by two trenches. Senden often enquired for the ruins of a temple of the god Thor, which he said was near Rotherham. This probably might be it, if we allow the name for any argument, besides, there is a pool not far from it called Jordon Dam, which name seems to be compounded of *Jor*, one of the names of the god *Thor*, and *Don*, the name of the river."

"If Brayton Bargh, Hambleton Hough, and Burton Bream were all in thy belly t'would never be team."

"So spoken of a covetous and insatiable person whom nothing will content. Brayton and Hambleton and Burton are places between Cawood and Pontefract, in this county. Brayton Bargh is a small hill in a plain country covered with wood. Bargh in the Northern dialect is properly a horse-way up a steep hill, though here it be taken for the hill itself."

"Many talk of Robin Hood that never shot in his bow,
And many talk of Little John that never did him know."

"Tales of Robin Hood are good enough for fools."

"That is, many talk of things which they have no skill in, or experience of. Robert Hood was a famous robber in the time of King Richard the First; his principal haunt was about *Shirewood* Forest, in Nottinghamshire. Camden calls him *prædonem mitissimum*. Of his stolen goods he afforded good penny-worths. Lightly come, lightly go."

"As freely as St. Robert gave his cow."

"This Robert was a Knaresburgh saint, and the old women there can still tell you the legend of the cow."

"As good as George of Green."

"This George of Green was that famous Pinder, of Wakefield, who fought with Robin Hood and Little John both together, and got the better of them, as the old ballad tells us. Called George a Green because he wore green bay in his hat."

"As blind as a mole,"

"'As blind as a mole,' though, indeed, a mole be not absolutely blind, but hath perfect eyes, and those not covered with a membrane as some have reported, but open and to be found outside the head if one search diligently, being very small and lying hid in the fur."

Darwin states that in some cases the eyes of moles are completely obscured by skin and fur. Many subterranean and cave-inhabiting animals are perfectly blind, having lost the eyes through disuse.

"A wooll-seller knows a wooll-buyer."

That is, that in Yorkshire the two are well matched for shrewdness. The cloth trade at Leeds is thus mentioned in an old work, date 1745:—
"Leeds on the Are is a wealthy large populous town; and upon account of its Cloth market may be called the principal place in the kingdom. The sale of cloth on the market days is prodigious; for it has two days, whereas Exeter has but one."

The following old Yorkshire weather proverbs, handed down to us probably from Saxon times, are still in common use :—

"A bushel of March dust is worth a King's ransom."

"When April blows his horn, it's good both for hay and corn."

That is, when it thunders in April.

"A May flood never did good."

"Look at your corn in May, and you'll come weeping away,
Look at the same in June, and you'll whistle a tune."

"A swarm of bees in May is worth a load of hay,
A swarm in July is not worth a fly."

"When the wind's in the east, it's neither good for man nor beast."

"A snow year, a rich year."

"A cloudy morning bodes a fair afternoon."

"The grey morning cheereth the traveller."

"An evening red and morning grey is a sure sign of a fine day."

"If there be a rainbow in the eve it will rain and leave; but if there be a rainbow in the morrow, it will neither lend nor borrow."

"When the clouds are upon the hills they'll come down by the mills."

"When the sloe tree's as white as a sheet,
Sow your barley whether it be dry or weet."

"A rainbow in the morning is the shepherd's warning,
A rainbow at night is the shepherd's delight."

"When the peacock loudly bawls,
Soon there'll be both rain and squalls."

"When rooks fly sporting high in air,
It shows that windy storms are near."

"If the moon shows like a silver shield,
Be not afraid to reap your field;
But if she rises haloed round,
Soon shall we tread on deluged ground."

Lofthouse. GEORGE ROBERTS

PERSONAL DISTINCTIONS AND TITLES.

N Anglo-Saxon times *Christian* names were only conferred on important persons, such as landowners and manorial lords. This is plainly shown in the Domesday Survey. During the Norman and Plantagenet rule *surnames* were added for purposes of distinction, of a local and topographical import, usually indicating the birth-place, place of abode, or adoption of the possessor—for instance, Adam de *Beeston*, William de *Rothwell*, Henry de *Wakefield*, appear in medieval deeds.

The common folk, who were virtually slaves and bondmen, and considered as mere goods and chattels, were of little account in the roll of humanity, and were classed as so many *villanes, bordarri*, or *cottarri*. Manual labour and handicraft trades were confined to them, employments viewed as menial by their superior lords, who were chiefly engaged in the pleasures of the chase and hawking, in preparatory exercises of chivalry or the sterner duties of war. When any member of the working-class became proficient in, or showed a special aptitude for a particular kind of workmanship or employment, as a distinguishing mark, and to avoid confusion, he was called after it, hence the common names of Taylor, Smith, Naylor, Farrer, Wright, Wainwright, Cartwright, and so on—patronymics perpetuated by their children and descendants.

As ideas of convenience or luxury grew, these people became increasingly necessary to their employers, from whom they received, in exchange for services rendered, payment in kind, agricultural produce, and in many instances grants of land, then held and valued by the grantors at so cheap a rate. In process of time this brought about the emancipation of their order, as the possession of land and wealth brings power. Trade guilds were formed, apprenticeships instituted, freedom conferred, trade ennobled, and commerce extended.

Others, were named after the feudal offices they filled, chiefly associated with the person or demesne of the lord, as examples, Archer, Parker (or park-keeper), Hunt, Grosvenour (great-hunter), Palfrey-man, Marshall (or horse-keeper), Vavasour—originally valvasour, a dignity below a baron and above a knight. In Norman times his duty was to keep ward, "ad valvas regni," at the gates, entrances, or borders of the realm; Ward, Forester, &c.

Some were designated from personal characteristics or physical ability, as *White*-head, *Broad*-head, *Red*-head, *Bird*-head, *Gawk*-roger, *Swift*, which names in the originals might be very suitable, but often became strangely inappropriate in their successors. Christian names, with the addition of *son*, were turned into surnames—a custom carried out in Wales and Lancashire to an almost ridiculous extent.

Others were known by the spot or locality in which they resided, for instance, *Roydhouse* (a dwelling in the wood-clearance), *Appleyard*, *Birkinshaw*, *Flockton*, *Kirkby* (near the church), &c.

Passing by the titles of nobility, the local historian, in examining old documents, searching through registers, or perusing tablets and tombstones, will often come across what may be termed inferior titles of distinction. These in former times were carefully noted and persistently maintained. They marked certain grades of society, and meant evidently more than they do at this day. Some were of feudal origin, some clerical or professional, others obtained or given by courtesy. We will begin with those of the highest degree, and attempt to describe their real significance. *Affixes* to the name—"*Miles*," a soldier, a knight, one who was connected with the military profession. Knighthood is not hereditary, but was and is conferred on the bearer for personal services or qualities. If given on the field of battle, the possessor has precedence before those not so created.

Armiger—the Latin name for armour-bearer—and *Esquier*—the shield-bearer, from the Norman French—seem to be equivalent. The person holding this title in chivalric days was generally a young man, of good birth, and attendant on a knight. This as a dignity was first conferred by Henry IV. and his successors, together with the investiture of the S.S. collar and the gift of a pair of silver spurs. By courtesy coroners and justices of the peace, and gentlemen of the Royal Household, barristers-at-law, doctors of divinity, law and medical, are entitled to this honour, but not tradespeople. Of course in later days these walls of distinction have been broken down.

"*Chivaler*,"—so spelled in the middle ages—signified horseman. It was a title of great honour and knightly import.

Genor—generosus, or gent, meaning gentleman. This title is rather more vague than the others, but it seems to belong to a person of good family, or descended from one which has long borne arms, the grant of which adds gentility to a man's family. It is often accompanied by the possession of wealth. The term is peculiarly English; it is associated with courteous manners and noble bearing, and in more modern times was of a higher standing than that of esquire.

Yeoman—was originally a Saxon who had never been under the Norman yoke, being a freeholder and farming his own land. Sir Thomas Smith defines a yeoman to be " a free-born Englishman, who may lay out of his own free land, in yearly revenue the sum of forty shillings." Some say that it signified at first yewman, from bearing the bow in battle, and, as a body guard, were thus powerful auxiliaries to the efforts of knights and esquires.

Prefixes to the name—MR.—magister, maister, master. This was a title of high respect, implying command and dignity. It was reserved for clergymen, barristers, and other persons of consequence. Persons holding official positions were designated " maisters." In a will dated 1522-3 Thomas Legh, of Middleton, Esq., it states—" I will that thir be giffyn to the ' church maisters ' of Rothwell, &c." (meaning church-wardens.)

SIR has lost some of its meaning, derived from sihor (Gothic), signifying lord or seigneur. It also came to signify all who had taken a degree or had entered into holy orders. For instance, as one of the witnesses in the above-mentioned will was " *Sir* " William Dey, parish priest of Rothwell. This likewise accounts for the abbreviation of *Dns* —dominus, lord—being placed before the names of certain vicars in olden time, as given in Torre's Close Catalogues. Thus, I presume, the above comments may be useful and interesting to the social student in endeavouring to get at the precise meanings of these titles, the qualifications required of the bearers, the duties enjoined, and the positions attached to them.

East Ardsley,   JOHN BATTY, F.R.H.S.

A CELEBRATED FAIR

ONE of the most remarkable of these annual gatherings will be well known to many Yorkshire readers, as well as to numbers residing beyond the county. We refer to " Lee Fair," held annually in August and September: and though the fair is now insignificant as compared with what it was centuries ago, it is still one of the most important in the West Riding. Though the place where this annual gathering is held is known in county records as West Ardsley, yet its two horse fairs, known as " t'first Lee " and " t'latter Lee," have given their name to the place as well, which is better known throughout Yorkshire as " Lee Fair " than by its proper title. These fairs are of very old date. Mr. Batty, in a paper on the Priory of St. Oswald at Nostel, says the Canons of Nostel received a charter from King Stephen to hold two annual fairs, but in the preface to the Woodkirk (or Wakefield) Mysteries (usually called the Towneley Mysteries) it is shown that King Henry I. made the original grant, and Stephen confirmed it. The days fixed are given as " Feast of the Assumption," and " Feast of the Nativity of the Blessed Mary," viz., 15th August and 8th September. How long these dates were adhered to we cannot determine, but the present fairs are nine days later, 24th August (St. Bartholomew's Day) and 17th September. Another important change has taken place with respect to these fairs, for, whereas, they are now only held on the two days last-named, a century ago there was in reality but one fair, which lasted for three weeks, and was one of the most important in the kingdom. It was at that time a mart for the sale of nearly all kinds of produce, as well as being celebrated for the size and importance

Arms of Nostel Priory.

144

of its transactions in horses and cattle. Fruit, onions, &c., were in abundance, and it is said that "multitudes came from towards Huddersfield, and many other parts of the county to purchase these articles, which then were stowed in barns, and sold at booths by lamplight in the morning." If we are to believe the testimony of the "oldest inhabitant," "Lee Fair" of fifty years ago was a gathering which once seen was ever remembered, having only its counterpart in the fun and frolic of "Donnybrook," in the sister isle. As to the origin of the name "Lee," Scatcherd derives it from the name of Dr. Legh, grantee of the site of Nostel Priory, in 1540. That the Legh family had connection with West Ardsley is shown in Thoresby's Duc. Leod., 221, in the Legh pedigree, where it names William Leghe, Esq., attainted 33 Henry VIII., as seized of lands in West Ardsley and Westerton. This person was attainted of high treason with Edward Tattersall, a clothier, and Ambler, a priest, and was executed in 1541. An interesting notice of "Lee Fair" is to be found in the court rolls of the manor of Wakefield, and therefrom something is learned about the scenes which took place at this annual carnival. Notwithstanding that the fair at that time belonged to the Canons of Wodekirk, riot and disorder were not uncommon :—

Alicia de Scardeby op. se versus Johannem de Heton, et quer: quod die Lunæ, in FESTO NATIVITATIS BEATÆ MARIÆ, anno regis Edwardi nunc nono, idem Johannes insultum fecit in ipsam, Aliciam et cepit, ipsam per capillos capitis sui in nundinis de Wodekirk, et ipsam extraxit per capillos prædictos, a parte boreali ex parte nunc prædict : quosque fossatum : Australi ex parte earundem. Et quia non potuit capillos predictos eridicare in hac forma, emarcuit ped, suo in facie ejusdem. Aliciæ causa eradicandi capillos predictos : et nihil hominus cepit quendam baculum et ipsam verberavit ultra humeros, lumbos, et corpus, et alia enormia et intultit, ad dampa sua C solet inde perduxit sectam.

The John de Heton named in this charge was the head of a great family living at Old Howley Hall, near Woodkirk. His wife Amabil was also concerned in this outrage, and complaint was made against both, and also against one John Graffard, in the same court. John de Heton was evidently a pugnacious character, for one John of Newcastle also complained of him for an assault and battery at the same fair, to his damage of 100 shillings; and one William (the) Carter also laid complaint that the said John de Heton had come into his stall at the fair and had overturned it, by which he lost 20 gallons of beer worth 2s. 4d., a cask value 12d., and a sack worth 8d. ; the covering of his stall was also torn, damage 12d., and other injuries ; total loss 40s.—a great sum of money in those days. One thing more in the above extract is noticeable, namely, the distance from whence people came to this very celebrated fair to lay in their stock of necessaries for the winter. Here we have two travellers, Alice (of) Scardeby and John of Newcastle— the one probably a thrifty housewife, and the other a dealer in cattle and wares. There is in this incident a fair illustration of how, in these ancient chivalrous times, the great men of the day conducted themselves. John de Heton, in all probability aided by his man Graffard and wife

Amabil, made valorous by the carter's good liquor, kicks up a row, overturns the landlord's stall, taps his casks, knocks down the Newcastle wight, and then falls foul upon the person of Alice de Scardeby. The fair at Woodkirk at this period (Edward II.) was reckoned amongst the most famous then held in the country, and to which it is said that merchants from France, Spain, Florence, the Low Countries, and even Germany came with their wares and merchandise to sell, and every family of consequence, as well as the religious houses, laid in their stock of necessaries for a whole year. In these accommodating days the priest and clerk stood ready all day, during the time of the fair, to marry in the neighbouring church all such as, during the mirth of the fair, were desirous to enter the matrimonial state. Another noteworthy circumstance connected with this celebrated fair must not be overlooked. On St. Bartholomew's Day, on which the fair ended, the scholars from the Grammar Schools of Leeds, Wakefield, and other places were brought to this place for disputation, or to ascertain their proficiency in classical learning, yearly down to the early part of last century. Whether these examinations were conducted on the Oxford and Cambridge models, or on that of the Science and Art department of the Yorkshire Union of Mechanics' Institutes, there is no authentic *data* on which to found an opinion; but St. Bartholomew, the patron or tutelary saint of scholars, held high carnival once a year at "Lee Fair." An amusing incident connected with one of these gatherings is related by an old man who died about 1780. He says "My father, when a boy, was present during a disputation, and had well-nigh been knocked on the head by a beadle, for happening to ask one of the boys who stood up improper questions, the gentleman in gold-laced robe and cocked hat applied his truncheon so forcibly to the ' pericranium ' of the catechiser as made him remember his impudence all his life afterwards." Readers of these pages will have learnt by this time not to judge of what Woodkirk Fair was, from what "Lee Fair" now is. In our own day it was of much more consequence than it has been for many years past, and musicians, actors, and jugglers, such as were brought to fairs to attract company, were present in large numbers.

Morley, near Leeds. THE EDITOR.

BISHOP BLAIZE FESTIVAL

BISHOP BLAIZE holds a place in the Calendar of the Church, but on what grounds antiquaries are unable to say. The fact that a tradition credits him with being the inventor of wool-combing is sufficient, however, to account for the maintenance of his reputation in England, and particularly in Yorkshire. It was known that he was Bishop of Sebaste, in Armenia, and that he was martyred under Licinius in 316. Ribadeneira relates that St. Blaize lived in a cave, whither wild beasts came daily to visit him, and be cured by him; "and, if it happened that they came while he was at prayer, they did not interrupt him, but waited till he had ended, and never departed without his benediction. He was discovered in his retirement, imprisoned, and cured a youth who had a fish-bone stuck in his throat, by praying." Ribadeneira further says St. Blaize was scourged, and seven holy women anointed themselves with his blood; whereupon their flesh was combed with iron combs, their wounds ran nothing but milk, and their flesh was whiter than snow, angels came visibly and healed their wounds as fast as they were made; and they were put into the fire, which would not consume them: wherefore they were ordered to be beheaded, and were beheaded accordingly. Then St. Blaize was ordered to be drowned in the lake; but he walked on the water, sat down, and invited the infidels to a sitting; whereupon three score and eight, who tried the experiment, were drowned, and St. Blaize walked back to be beheaded.

A full-sized representation of the Bishop is carved in stone at the principal entrance of the Bradford Exchange. The wool-staplers of the town have not ceased to keep green the memory of their patron, but the great septennial festivals provided by them in honour of the Bishop have long since lapsed by default. In the *Leeds Mercury* of the 5th of February, 1825, is an account of the last celebration of this festival, held in Bradford two days previously. This account furnishes the very interesting particulars in the subjoined account:—

There is no place in the kingdom where the Bishop is so splendidly commemorated as at Bradford. In 1811, 1818, and at previous septennial periods, the occasion was celebrated with great pomp and festivity, each celebration surpassing the preceding ones in number and brilliance. The celebration of 1825 eclipsed all hitherto seen, and it is most gratifying to know that this is owing to the high prosperity of the worsted and woollen manufactures, which are constantly adding fresh streets and suburban villages to the town. The different trades began to assemble at eight o'clock in the morning, but it was near ten o'clock before they were all arranged in marching order in Westgate. The arrangements were actively superintended by Matthew Thompson, Esq. The morning was brilliantly beautiful. As early as seven o'clock, strangers poured into Bradford from the surrounding towns and villages, in such numbers as to line the road in every direction; and almost all the vehicles within twenty miles were in requisition. Bradford was never before known to be so crowded with strangers. Many thousands of individuals must have come to witness the scene. About ten o'clock the procession was drawn up in the following order:—

Herald bearing a flag.
Woolstaplers on horseback, each horse caparisoned
with a fleece.
Worsted Spinners and Manufacturers on horseback, in white stuff
waistcoats, with each a sliver over the shoulder, and a
white stuff sash, the horses' necks covered
with nets made of thick yarn.

Merchants on horseback, with coloured sashes.
Three Guards. Masters' colours. Three Guards.
Apprentices and Masters' Sons on horseback, with ornamented
caps, scarlet stuff coats, white stuff waistcoats,
and blue pantaloons.
Bradford and Keighley Bands.
Mace-bearer, on foot.
Six Guards. KING. QUEEN. Six Guards.
Guards. JASON. PRINCESS MEDEA. Guards.
Bishop's Chaplain.
BISHOP BLAIZE.
Shepherd and Shepherdess.
Shepherd Swains.
Woolsorters on horseback, with ornamented caps and
various coloured slivers.
Comb Makers.
Charcoal Burners.
Combers' Colours.
Band.
Woolcombers, with wool wigs, &c.
Band.
Dyers, with red cockades, blue aprons, and crossed slivers of
red and blue.

The following were the numbers of the different bodies, as nearly as could be estimated :—24 *woolstaplers*, 38 *spinners and manufacturers*, 6 *merchants*, 56 *apprentices and masters' sons*, 160 *woolsorters*, 30 *combmakers*, 470 *woolcombers*, and 40 *dyers*. The KING, on this occasion, was an old man, named WM. CLOUGH, of Darlington, who had filled the regal station at four previous celebrations. JASON (the celebrated legend of the Golden Fleece of Colchis, is interwoven with the commemoration of the Bishop,) was personated by JOHN SMITH ; and the fair MEDEA, to whom he was indebted for his spoils, rode by his side.—BISHOP BLAIZE was a personage of very becoming gravity, also named JOHN SMITH ; and he had enjoyed his pontificate on several previous commemorations ; his chaplain was JAMES BEETHAM. The ornaments of the spinners and manufacturers had a neat and even elegant appearance, from the delicate and glossy whiteness of the finely combed wool which they wore. The apprentices and masters' sons, however, formed the most showy part of the procession, their caps being richly adorned with ostrich feathers, flowers, and knots of various coloured yarn, and their stuff garments being of the gayest colours ; some of these dresses, we understand, were very costly, from the profusion of their decorations. The shepherd, shepherdess, and swains were attired in light green. The woolsorters, from their number, and the height of their plumes of feathers, which were, for the most part, of different colours, and formed in the shape of *fleur-de-lys*, had a most dashing appearance. The combmakers carried before them the instruments here so much celebrated, raised on standards, together with golden fleeces, rams' heads with gilded horns, and other emblems. The combers looked both neat and comfortable in their flowing wigs of well-combed wool ; and the garb of the dyers was quite professional

Several well-painted flags were displayed, one of which represented on one side the venerable BISHOP *in full robes*, and on the other a shepherd and shepherdess under a tree. Another had a painting of MEDEA *giving up the golden fleece* to JASON; a third had a portrait of the KING; and a fourth appeared to belong to some association in the trade. The whole procession was from half a mile to a mile in length.

When the procession was ready to move, *Richard Fawcett, Esq.*, who was on horseback at the head of the spinners, pronounced, uncovered, and with great animation, the following lines, which it had long been customary to repeat on these occasions, and which, if they have not much poetical elegance, have the merit of expressing true sentiments in simple language:—

>Hail to the day, whose kind auspicious rays
>Deign'd first to smile on famous Bishop Blaize!
>To the great author of our combing trade,
>This day's devoted, and due honour's paid;
>To him whose fame thro' Britain's isle resounds,
>To him whose goodness to the poor abounds.
>Long shall his name in British annals shine,
>And grateful ages offer at his shrine:
>By this our trade are thousands daily fed,
>By it supplied with means to earn their bread,
>In various forms our trade its work imparts,
>In different methods, and by different arts;
>Preserves from starving indigents distress'd,
>As combers, spinners, weavers, and the rest.
>We boast no gems, or costly garments vain,
>Borrowed from India, or the coast of Spain:—
>Our native soil with wool our trade supplies,
>While foreign countries envy us the prize.
>No foreign broil our common good annoys,
>Our country's product all our art employs;
>Our fleecy flocks abound in every vale,
>Our bleating lambs proclaim the joyful tale.
>So let not Spain with us attempt to vie,
>Nor India's wealth pretend to soar so high;
>Nor Jason pride him in his Colchian spoil,
>By hardships gained, and enterprising toil,
>Since Britons all with ease attain the prize,
>And every hill resounds with golden cries.
>To celebrate our founder's great renown,
>Our shepherd and our shepherdess we crown;
>For England's commerce, and for George's sway,
>Each loyal subject give a loud Hurra! Hurra!

These lines were afterwards several times repeated in the principal streets and roads through which the cavalcade passed. About five o'clock they dispersed.

A representation of the jubilee is given in one of the plates to the "Costumes of Yorkshire" (4to, 1814), and this work states the order of the procession to be as follows:—" The masters on horseback; with each a white sliver; the masters' sons on horseback; their colours; the apprentices on horseback, in their uniforms; music; the King and Queen; the royal family; their guards and attendants; Jason; the golden fleece; attendants; Bishop and Chaplain; their attendants; shepherd and shepherdess; shepherd's swains, attendants, &c.; foremen and woolsorters on horseback; combers' colours; woolcombers, two and two; wool wigs and various coloured slivers."

Brand states that Minshew, in his dictionary, under the word "Hock-tide," speaks of St. Blaize—"His day about Candlemas, when country women go about and make goode cheere; and if they find any of their neighbour women a spinning that day, they burne and make a fire of the distaffe, and thereof called S. Blaze, his day." Dr. Percy, in his notes to the "Northumberland Household Book" (p. 333), states—"The anniversary of St. Blazius is the 3rd of February, when it is still the custom in many parts of England to light up fires on the hills on St. Blayse night—a custom anciently taken up, perhaps, for no better reason than the jingling resemblance of the name to the word blaze."

FIELD KIRK FAIR

This is only a corruption of "Field Cock Fair," by which name it was known when the writer was a boy attending the Grammar School at Batley, or rather making himself acquainted with all the places of local interest lying between Morley and the school, of which places Lady Anne's Well, Howley Hall, and other well-known resorts came in for more attention on his part than grammar, arithmetic, or the classics. The fair had its origin, in all probability, from a religious custom. "Fairs," says Scatcherd, "were anciently held in churchyards on the day of the dedication of their respective churches," or on the Sunday following. According to Saxon laws, the ranks of ecclesiastical structures were as follows:—First, the Minster or mother church; secondly, the church having a place of burial; thirdly, the field-kirk or chapel without cemetery. In Saxon and early Norman times *the* church of the parish in which Howley was situated was at Morley, and afterwards at Batley. There are vestiges of some place of worship at Howley, and this, in all likelihood, was a mere parochial chapel, called in those days a "Field Kirk," important enough, however, to give rise to a village wake or fair, which would naturally be called "Field Kirk Fair." We have also at or near to Howley a "Holy Well," which also was a place of annual resort. Here, then, in the vicinity of Howley Hall, we have two religious edifices in early times—the Kirk of Batley, and the Chapel, or Field Kirk, at Howley or Southwell. "Can any one doubt," says Scatcherd, "that there was here in former days a fair? Ask, then, a villager returning from the annual assemblage where he has been, and he will reply: 'I have been to Fieldcock Fair.' This is the only name by which it goes; but who can doubt that it is a corruption of Field Kirk Fair?" Much interesting information concerning this and similar fairs, and well-worship generally, may be gathered from pages 254-9 of "Scatcherd's History of Morley."

Morley, near Leeds.   The Editor.

WATERTON, THE WANDERER

CHARLES WATERTON was born at Walton Hall, near Wakefield, in 1782. He was the representative of one of the most ancient untitled families in England, of Saxon origin, a knightly race, which, prior to the Reformation, had numbered among its members many eminent holders of high offices of State, tracing their descent from several Royal families, and, through the grandmother of Charles Waterton, from Sir Thomas More, of which he was exceedingly proud. The family adhered to the old faith at the Reformation, and suffered greatly in consequence, both in estate and by persecution. They were also Royalists during the Civil war, when they were again great pecuniary sufferers. Walton Hall at that time underwent a siege, and in the old gateway there is shown a bullet, which is said by tradition to have been shot by Cromwell. Charles himself was not a whit behind any of his ancestors in his devotion to the old Catholic faith, and in his adherence to the exiled Stuarts, which are shown by sarcastic references, scattered through his writings, to Luther, Henry VIII., Cranmer, Queen Bess, Cromwell, Dutch William, the Hanoverian Rats, &c.

The Watertons were originally Lords of the Manor of Waterton, in Lincolnshire; but in the reign of Richard II., Sir John Waterton acquired Walton by marriage with the heiress of the De Burghs, and became Lord of the Manor of Methley, in exchange for some advowsons, which latter passed by marriage to the Barons Welles, and from them to the Saviles. Walton Hall, which belonged at the Conquest to Ashenwold, a Saxon Thegn, was given to Ilbert de Lacy, and formed part of his Honor of Pontefract, which he granted back in fief to Ailric, son of Ashenwold. The old family house, built a thousand years ago, was a fine castellated building, with a noble wainscoted hall, 90 feet long, where the Watertons for many centuries banqueted with their friends and drunk the healths of Philip and Mary, the Charleses and Jameses, and the King "over the water," and denounced Henry, the sacrilegous tyrant, the heretic Bess, the Miller of Huntingdon, the Dutch usurper, and the Hanoverian Rats. Becoming decayed, it was taken down by Charles Waterton's father, who built the existing ugly mansion in its place, leaving only, on the edge of the lake, a picturesque old gateway, with a central and two flanking towers, covered with ivy, the abode of colonies of birds, often referred to by Waterton in his essays.

Walton Hall.

The Hall stood in the midst of an extensive park, picturesquely undulating, with a fine lake and groups of majestic trees, which, under the hands of the naturalist, became a perfect menagerie, a veritable Noah's ark of birds, beasts, and fishes, with all sorts of buildings and contrivances for their comfort and convenience, and which he surrounded with a wall at a cost of £10,000 to protect them from marauders. The Hall also became a perfect museum of stuffed birds and animals collected in his travels, which were all prepared by his own hands or under his direction by methods devised by himself, so as to display their natural characteristics. He was educated at Tudhoe school, now Ushaw College, and at Stonyhurst under the Jesuit Fathers. There he got into many a scrape by breaking bounds to go naturalising

In 1827, he married Annie Mary, daughter of Chas. Edmonstone, of Demerara, by Helen, daughter of William Reid and Minie, an Indian "Princess" of the Arowak tribe. Her father was descended from Sir John Edmondstone, who married Isabel, daughter of King Robert Bruce. She died the following year in giving birth to her only son Edmund, and Waterton never again married. His life was one continuous series of romantic adventures, daring exploits, and perils. On leaving college he was sent to Spain, where he had two uncles engaged in commercial pursuits. He was in Malaga when a fearful plague—the black vomit—broke out with great virulence, 14,000 people dying of it, whilst 50,000 fled from the city. His two uncles died of it, and he caught the infection, but thanks to a good constitution, he became convalescent, when, fearing a relapse, and an earthquake occurring, he determined to escape from the doomed city, which he was enabled to do by the friendliness of a Swedish captain, who admitted him secretly on board his vessel. It got wind, however, that a plague patient was in the vessel, and two brigs of war went in pursuit; but the superior sailing powers of the Swede enabled it to outstrip its pursuers, and Waterton landed safely in England, but was several months before he completely recovered.

He was then sent to superintend a family estate on the Demerara river, in British Guiana, where he remained eight years, when his father and uncle having died, he handed it over to the heirs. Whilst there he was commissioned to carry some despatches to the Spanish Government on the Oronoko, his commission, dated August, 1808, being the first held by a Waterton since the time of Queen Mary. This was the commencement of his wanderings as a naturalist. He made four voyages to America—in 1812, 1816, 1820, and 1824, the last year, however, being occupied chiefly with a tour through the United States; the others almost exclusively in the forests of the Demerara and the Essequibo, which he ranged fearlessly, dressed only in a shirt, a pair of trousers, and a hat. He went barefoot, carrying with him a gun to provide food and enable him to obtain specimens of rare and new animals. He wrote—"There is not much danger in roving among snakes and wild animals, if you only have self-command. You must not approach them abruptly; if you do you will have to pay for your rashness. They will always retire from the face of man unless pressed by hunger or suspicious of an attack, as in case of a serpent being trodden upon. Their dominant idea is that of self-defence, and it is only when alarmed that the jaguar knocks you down with his paw, or the snake brings his fangs into operation." .He seemed to care little for jaguars, alligators, and serpents, however big or ferocious, his great annoyance arising from much more insignificant creatures, viz., the myriads of pestiferous insects of all sizes and shapes, most particularly the chigoe, about the size of a flea, which burrowed under the toenails and there deposited its bag of eggs, which had to be extracted by means of a needle or penknife without breaking the bag, and turpentine poured into the wound, else would the young chigoes, when hatched, burrow still further, and cause an ulcerated sore and eventually the loss of the foot. On some occasions he extracted as many as four bags of eggs from his toes in a day.

He had many narrow escapes from death; for instance, he was passing down a river in a canoe, when he saw a huge Laboris snake— a powerful and deadly poisonous creature—on the bank. He wounded it with a gunshot, and caused the canoe to be brought up to the bank, in order to secure his specimen. He laid hold of a branch, and was preparing to grasp it by the throat, when the tillerman, terrified at the aspect of the snake, turned the boat off, and left Waterton swinging from the branch, half in the water, and thrice going overhead in the river, which swarmed with caymen. Another man, however, seized the helm and brought the boat back, and he was rescued from his perilous position. Determined not to lose his prize, he seized it by the neck, dragged it into the boat, and despatched it.

He had another adventure with a snake. This time a Couracalle, not poisonous, but thick and muscular, and 14 feet in length. He was anxious to get it perfect without wounding the skin by a shot, which he thought he could do by pinning it through the neck to the earth—a difficult thing to achieve, as it was lying coiled up under some woodbine which had grown over the roots of an old tree, and the head was not visible. He had two negroes with him, who were terribly alarmed at the project, and prayed that he would shoot it. Knowing that their first impulse would be flight, he told them that he would cutlass them if they did not stand by him in the struggle. He then approached silently, and gently kneeling on one knee, cut away the woodbine until the head appeared. This took a quarter of an hour to accomplish. He ranged the negroes behind him, one to seize and firmly hold the lance after the blow had been given, the other to wait his instructions. "Probably," says he, "nothing kept them from bolting but the consolation that I was betwixt them and the snake." They then, in dead silence, approached the reptile, which had not moved; "and on getting up to him, I struck him with the lance on the near side, just behind the neck, and pinned him to the ground. That moment the negro nearest me seized the lance, and held it firm in its place, while I dashed head foremost into the den to grapple with the snake, and to get hold of his tail before he could do any mischief. On pressing him to the ground he gave a tremendous loud hiss, and the little dog ran away, howling as he went. We had a sharp fray in the den, rotten sticks flying about in all directions. I called up the second negro to throw himself upon me, as I found I was not heavy enough. He did so, and the additional weight was of good service. I had now got good hold of his tail, and after a violent struggle he gave in. This was the moment to secure him, so while the first negro held the lance firm to the ground, the other was helping me to tie up his mouth. The snake now finding himself in an unpleasant situation, tried to better himself, and set resolutely to work, but we overpowered him. We contrived to make him twist himself round the lance, and then prepared to convey him from the forest. I stood at the head, and held it under my arm; one negro supported the body, and the other the tail, but he was so heavy that we had to rest ten times to recover our strength. As we proceeded he fought hard for freedom, but it was all in vain. Had I killed him partial putrefaction would have taken place before morning." When they reached the hut, they put him in a large sack, securely tying the mouth, and placed him in the basement room. "My hammock was in the loft just above him, and the floor betwixt us half gone to decay, so that in parts of it, no boards intervened between his lodging-room and mine. He was very restless and fretful, and, had Medusa been my wife, there could not have been more continuous and disagreeable hissing in the bed-chamber that night. In the morning ten negroes were sent for to prevent his escape on opening the bag. We untied the mouth of the bag, kept him down by main force, and then I cut his throat. He bled like an ox, and by six the same evening he was completely dissected."

On another occasion he found a young Couracalle, ten feet long, which he irritated by seizing its tail, when it turned and came at him open-mouthed; but he dashed his hand covered with his cap into its throat, and grasping it by the neck, let go its tail, when it coiled itself round his body, "pressing me hard, but not alarmingly so; and so I marched off with my prize."

The famous cayman ride, which gave rise to so much derision from the critics, occurred in his third journey, on the Essequibo river. He was anxious to procure a specimen uninjured by shot, and went accompanied by Daddy Quashi, his faithful negro, and some others—Indians and negroes. They found a cayman ten and a half feet long, which they vainly tried to catch, until an Indian constructed a hook and bait, which was laid overnight, attached to a strong rope, the other end of which was fastened to a post driven into the bank. In the morning they found that he had swallowed the bait and was tugging at the rope. Waterton wished to draw him out alive, but the Indians declared that he would worry them; and Daddy Quashi, terribly afraid, prepared his gun to shoot. This was only prevented by his master threatening him with a knife. Waterton walked up and down some time, revolving in his mind various projects, then sent for the boat mast, eight feet long, round which he wrapped the sail, and kneeling down with it projecting before him, gave orders to haul away. After some plunging and splashing, the cayman was brought to the bank. "By this time he was within two yards of me; I saw he was in a state of fear and perturbation, so I dropped the mast, which I intended to ram down his throat, and jumped on his back, turning half round as I vaulted, so that I gained my seat, with my face in a right position. I immediately seized his fore legs, and by main force twisted them on his back; thus they served me for a bridle. He now seemed to have recovered from his surprise, and probably fancying himself in hostile company, began to plunge furiously, and lashed the sand with his long and fearful tail. He continued to plunge and strike, and made my seat very uncomfortable. It must have been a fine sight for an unoccupied spectator. The people roared out in triumph, and it was some time before they heard me tell them to pull me and my beast of burthen farther inland. I was apprehensive the rope might break, and then there would have been every chance of going down to the regions under water with him. We were dragged forty yards inland. Should it be asked how I managed to keep my seat, I would answer—I hunted some years ago with Lord Darlington's foxhounds. When by exhaustion he became a little tranquil, I managed to tie up his jaws and secure firmly his fore legs over his back. I then worked myself back upon his tail to prevent his kicking up a dust with it. The people then ventured near, conveyed him to the boat, and from it to the hammock, where his throat was cut." He was then dissected, and Daddy Quashi feasted on the flesh, declaring that it revived him wonderfully, and becoming very bold and talkative now that the danger was over.

He employed himself on his first journey in collecting specimens of the deadly Wourali poison prepared by the Indians for tipping their arrows with, and in experimenting on its effects on various animals. None survived more than ten or twelve minutes after it mingled with their blood. In the second he describes the varieties of resplendent humming birds of Guiana, "darting through the air as quick as thought, now within a yard of your face; in an instant flashing through the air and fluttering from flower to flower to sip the silver dew; now a ruby, now a topaz, now an emerald, now all burnished gold." He also descants in doleful tones on the cruelty and impolicy of the banishment of the Jesuit Fathers from Pernambuco, where they had established schools and colleges, and were the disseminators of learning and civilisation.

In the third journey occurred the cayman adventure, and his close observation of the habits of the sloth. He spent eleven months in the forest, and brought home 230 birds, two land tortoises, five armadilloes, two large serpents, a sloth, a cayman, an ant-bear, and a vast number of hitherto unknown insects.

On his return he visited Switzerland and Italy, and whilst in Rome climbed up the lightning conductor and left his glove on the top; but as this would impede its action, he was compelled by the authorities to make another ascent and remove it.

He was inspired to make his fourth and last journey by reading Wilson's "Ornithology of the United States," and passed through the States on his road to Guiana. He does not, however, give many notes on natural history, occupying his pages chiefly with compliments on the Americans, their cities, and institutions.

After all his dangers abroad, he died in consequence of a fall in his own park in 1865. He had previously chosen a spot for his burial in the midst of his pet birds and beasts, and there he had placed a stone cross inscribed, " Orate pro anima Caroli Waterton, cujus ossa—juxta hanc crucem—sepeliuntur ossa. Natus 1782; obiit 1865." When lying on his deathbed the Pope telegraphed a blessing. Charles Waterton's funeral was conducted by the Bishop of Beverley, assisted by fourteen priests. The procession, after Requiem High Mass at the house, passed along the lake in boats, draped in black, and when the benediction canticle was being sung over him, after the coffin had been deposited in the grave, a linnet in an overhanging tree lifted up its voice and with great appropriateness sang sweetly in unison with the choristers. In 1870 his collections in Natural History were sold by auction, along with his valuable library, pictures, coins, medals, and other works of art and objects of curiosity.

London. F. Ross, F.R.H.S.

JACK HAWLEY

LIONEL SCOTT PILKINGTON, *alias* Jack Hawley, of Hatfield, near Doncaster, was an eccentric character. Although born a gentleman and well educated, he chose to disguise himself in the dress, manners, pursuits, and speech of a much inferior class, associating with grooms and farm labourers, clothing himself in corduroy breeches, sleeved waistcoat, top boots, and fur cap, and speaking the dialect of the district in the broadest style. Yet beneath this rough and homely exterior he possessed the instincts of the gentleman. He was educated at Rugby, under the future Archbishop of Canterbury, was well read, possessing a large library, and was a careful reader of newspapers to keep abreast with the topics of the day, although he was wont to say, " I don't believe half of the stuff they put in newspapers; still there is as much truth in a newspaper as there is gospel in a sermon." He was also fond of studying animals and their habits, had an aviary in his drawing-room, and tame foxes which had the run of the house. He was free and generous in his disposition, kept a hospitable table, was affable in his demeanour, and had many friends, and few (if any) enemies. His father, Redman Pilkington, was an architect at Kensington and J.P. for the county of Middlesex, who purchased a considerable estate at Hatfield, near the mansion of his brother, Henry Pilkington. Lionel, his son, was born at Kensington, in 1828, and died at Hatfield, in 1875. After leaving Rugby he was sent by his father on his travels, with a private tutor; but as soon as he got across the Channel he refused to learn any more lessons, and would not consent to go any further, excepting in the capacity of servant to his tutor. When they reached Italy, he ran off, and was not found till six weeks afterwards, when he was discovered in a farm-house, where he had hired himself out as a day labourer. Afterwards, he entered the service of the Duke of Parma as a groom. His father died suddenly, and was buried in Hatfield Church, where there is a tablet to his memory; and as he made no will, his son, then a minor, succeeded to the estate and made it his residence, with a few short intervals, for the remainder of his life. He built a house on the estate, in a somewhat bizarre style, with antique lozenge-paned windows, and fire-hearths without ranges, on which he burnt turf, peat, or logs of wood. The floors of the rooms were carpeted with skins of animals, and the walls decorated with antlers, stuffed animals, and fox brushes; also with bits, bridles, and stirrups; portraits of favourite horses, and one of his great grandfather in the costume of a jockey. Outside were commodious stables and extensive greenhouses for the cultivation of exotic flowers.

He claimed to be a Catholic in religion, and on one occasion presented two fine horses to the Pope, who in return gave him a silver cross, which he had blessed, and which Lionel highly valued and wore suspended round his neck, day and night, until he accidentally lost it. He always made the sign of the cross, with great seriousness, when mounting or dismounting from his horse, Anglican. "Parsons" he had very little love for, and churchwardens were his especial abhorrence. This arose partly out of a quarrel he had had with the Vicar and churchwardens of Hatfield. The church was undergoing some alterations and repairs, and it was found necessary to remove the coffins of his grandfather and grandmother to a new vault. Amongst other repairs was some new lead spouting, and he was led to believe that it was made out of the coffins of his progenitors, whereupon he tore down the spouts, called the churchwardens "villains and scoundrels," and the Vicar a "thief and body-snatcher," supplemented by other choice epithets of a groom's vocabulary, for which breaches of the peace he was summoned before the West Riding magistrates and punished with a fine. He asserted, but it is supposed without truth, that when in Italy he married and had three children, and that when he left he handed them over to another man, which, he said, was sanctioned by the law of the land.

Multitudinous are the stories and anecdotes told of his adventures, frolics, and eccentricities, which show that he was always ready for a "lark," and that he possessed an abundance of mother wit, appreciation of humour, and kindliness of disposition, and that he was ever ready at repartee. Soon after his father's death, he made a voyage to India as a man before the mast, but that one voyage was sufficient for him; he never went to sea again excepting on a coasting trip. On his return he took service as a stableman at the Turf Inn, Doncaster, without wages; whence he passed to the stables of John Scott, the trainer, at Malton; afterwards became assistant to a butcher, at Barnby-upon-Dun, and subsequently passed, for a long period, into the service of Sir Joseph Hawley, of turf celebrity, which was the cause of his assuming the name of "Jack Hawley." On one occasion he took a harvesting job, but spent considerably more than his wages in beer for his fellow-labourers. Interspersed with these periods of service, he indulged in all sorts of mad-cap and grotesque frolics and amusements, generally of a "horsey" character. He had a presentiment that his death would take place on Christmas Day, which really occurred on December 25th, 1875. As he found his end approaching, he prepared for the future by causing his groom Harris to read portions of the Scriptures to him every evening, and made his will for the disposition of his property, with special directions for his funeral, and a condition that his legatees should see them carried out strictly, under the penalty of forfeiting their legacies. His Hatfield property he left to his then groom, John Harris; his London property to a young man named Wiggins, the son of an old and faithful servant of his mother, who still lived, and to whom the legatee was to pay the yearly sum of £50. To an old servant named Nettleship he left £25; to the Catholic priest of Doncaster a legacy of £25, and £5 per annum for masses for his soul; and to the Catholic Church at Doncaster, towards the building of which he had contributed liberally, a painting of the Virgin.

The funeral was carried out in accordance with his instructions. He had appropriated a field as a cemetery for rinderpest cattle, of which he lost several in the plague of 1870, favourite horses, foxes, dogs, cats, etc., and had left in the centre a vacant place for his own grave, where he placed a ponderous stone coffin for the receipt of his corpse. His body was clothed in his usual costume of white cord breeches, top-boots with silver-mounted spurs, a cut-away riding coat, and a sealskin cap decorated with a portion of the brush of a fox. His hands were crossed on his breast holding a crucifix and a bouquet of flowers, for which he had a great admiration, placed on his chest. The body was strapped on a board, and covered with a horse-rug, and was borne from the house by six men. In the coffin was placed a saddle for his pillow, with the bridle of his favourite pony at his feet. When the body was laid in its place, the massive lid of the coffin was lowered by means of a crane, and cemented down by the masons. Upon it was inscribed, " John Hawley, died December 25, 1875, aged 47 years." And thus terminated the career of this estimable and well-meaning, if wild and erratic, Yorkshireman.

London. F. Ross, F.R.H.S.

ANCIENT GRAVE STONES

IN writing of these specimens of Archæology to be found in Yorkshire we shall divide them into three classes, namely, incised cross slabs, raised cross slabs, and head crosses. By incised cross slabs is meant flat recumbent gravestones which have a cross or other Christian symbol incised upon them. By raised cross slabs is meant recumbent gravestones, whether flat or coped, which have upon them a cross or other symbol in bas-relief. These two classes have many features in common, especially in their designs. Head crosses are monumental stones, ornamented with crosses or symbols, either incised or in relief, placed upright or at the head of the grave.

Of the incised cross slabs, we find early specimens in the Vatican at Rome, these being found in the Roman Catacombs. Nearly all these stones bear an incised cross or other Christian emblem; some have in addition an inscription, others an emblem of the trade of the deceased, etc., and many of them remind one of the common English grave stones of the thirteenth, fourteenth and fifteenth centuries.

By going from one country to another we can obtain a connected series of these Christian gravestones from the time of the Apostles to the present day. The series in the Vatican extends from A.D. 89 to A.D. 400. The next in order of date are in Ireland, which bring down the series to the eleventh century. After this time the series is completed down to the present time from English examples.

In Yorkshire we have a fourteenth century specimen at York, which was found on the site of the Carmelite Friary. These crosses, formed of vine branches, are probably in allusion to the words of our Lord " I am the Vine, etc." Here the vine running through the chalice beautifully symbolizes the idea that the chalice was filled with the juice of that vine.

In the fifteenth century, we have an example from Kirkwood. In England we find cross slabs most abundant in stony districts, as in the northern counties, and in Derbyshire, and we find them of all kinds of stone, alabaster, Purbeck marble, granite, free-stone, lime-stone, etc. The ancient Christian modes of interment were in a cist or stone coffin, in one of lead or of wood, or in the earth without coffin. Some of the incised crosses doubtless formed the lids of stone coffins; but the greater number appear to have been used as monuments and coverings for the graves when other modes of interment were used. Wooden coffins were used very early; remains of them, with the iron clamps by which they have been fastened together, have been found in barrows; for instance, in the barrow called Lamel Hill, near York, which is made out by Dr. Thurman to be of Saxon date.* A curious example of an early wood coffin formed of a hollow oak trunk is preserved in the Museum at Scarborough.

Lead coffins too were in very early use, but were used sparingly until the end of the fourteenth century when they became more general. These coffins were sometimes enclosed in a wooden chest or coffin, sometimes in a stone chest or altar-tomb, surmounted by an effigy, or monumental brass.

The designs in both incised floor-crosses and coffin stones very much resemble one another; it will be convenient having first treated of peculiarites of coffin-stones, then to treat of the designs of both together.

The cist of many stones which has frequently been found in cairns or tumuli of stones, and also in the soil, and which has generally been attributed to the British inhabitants of the island, may be considered as a species of rude stone coffin.

Cross Carmelite Friary, York.

In Swinton Park, Yorkshire, are two valuable examples of early cists; one—like the proper stone coffin—has the base narrower than the top, and its lid is coped: the other

---

* Archæological Journal, Vol. 5, p. 38,

has the lid rounded at the sides and ends, and flat at the top, like a flat-bottomed boat* Mr. Tucker states that these belong to the end of the Romano-British period.

The sides of the coffin were sometimes ornamented, and it appears that the coffin was then placed above ground, as in the fine example from Coningsborough, whose front is covered with bas-reliefs. The sculpture on the front and lid of the coffin appear to be emblematical: a dragon which is trampling upon one man is opposed by a knight with sword and shield; behind the knight is a bishop in the usual attitude of benediction. It is not unlikely that the knight may represent the person whose monument this is, and the whole sculpture may represent some particular event in his life, or generally his zeal in defence of the Church. On the lid are two knights tilting; the temptation of Eve; and other sculptures which appear to be the signs of the zodiac. The costume and style of the work is that of the beginning of the twelfth century.

No raised cross slabs remain of so great antiquity as some of the incised cross slabs, though if we may include the two cist lids from Swinton in our list of coffin-lids, we arrive probably at a period as early as the fifth century.

Coningsborough.

In the two examples from Bedale,† we find the curious semi-circular or arched stones, which were probably placed over the grave, perhaps over the cist; these are perhaps of the eighth or ninth century, or even earlier. Most probably they are of Saxon workmanship. The first three cuts represent the bases of two sides, and one gabled end of the fragment of a stone found in the Choir of Bedale Church; the slope of the sides is sculptured to represent a roof covered with diamond-shaped tiles, as in the fragment figured in the fourth cut.

* For Engravings of these, see Archæological Journal, Vol. 5, p. 46.

The fourth cut represents one side of a fragment of a similar stone found in the same place; the gabled end of this fragment is plain.

A stone of similar character to the one at Bedale was discovered at the Church of St. Dionys, York; here too the section of the stone is arched rather than coped, at the junction of the arch with the sides and along the ridge runs a kind of cable moulding; one side has animals in low relief which appear to have some symbolical meaning, the other side is covered with dragon-like monsters, with wings, tails, etc., going off into the intricate interlaced work, so commonly found in the illuminations of early Anglo-Saxon MSS. Its date may be the seventh or eighth century.

An interesting stone of a somewhat similar character to the last-

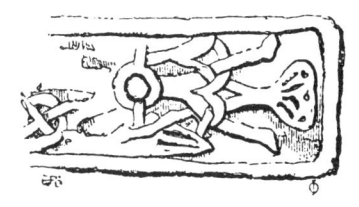

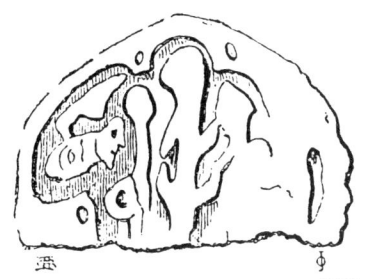

Arched Stones, Bedale.

named, is met with at Dewsbury.* Gough conjectures that the birds on this slab are eagles, and that the stone may be connected with the family of Soothill, whose cognizance was an eagle. The double calvary steps here are singular; the date of the stone is probably late in the twelfth century.

In the thirteenth century, as also in the succeeding centuries, we still find all shapes of the raised cross slab, both flat and coped. It is however, somewhat remarkable that while in all other parts of ecclesiastical architecture during the thirteenth, fourteenth and fifteenth centuries, we find three strongly marked styles, the early English, decorated, and perpendicular, we do not find any corresponding broad distinctions of style in gravestones. Ornamental work peculiar to these styles frequently occurs upon them, but almost as frequently there is so little of peculiar character in the design, that it requires considerable familiarity with the subject to be able to assign, within a hundred years, the probable date of a slab within this period.

When stone coffins went out of fashion about the end of the fifteenth century, the coffin-shaped stone still continued in common use as a covering to the grave, with little or no alteration in its shape or dimensions.

There is a variety of the simple highly-coped coffin lid, which is sometimes met with: viz., where instead of one simple ridge, there are two crossing one another at right angles, giving the idea of the roof of a cross church. The ridges are finished with a bold roll, so that the two rolls crossing at right angles form the symbol of the cross, as at Fingall, Yorkshire.

Double coffin stones also occur having two crosses upon them, as at Goosenerg,* in the County of Lancaster, the crosses having each a shield at the base and other ornamental work. Each compartment of this singular stone contains a cross, the spaces between the shafts and border being filled in with trefoils, etc. The letters A.R. are of comparatively modern date, the stone having been used a second time. The border is filled with the common four-leaved flower of the fourteenth century.

Sometimes the cross was omitted, and we have only the head within a quatrefoil, though indeed the quatrefoil itself forms a cross. Sometimes the head of the cross is expanded into a large quatrefoil in which the upper part of the deceased is represented, and the base of the cross into a trefoil where the feet appear as in the

Slab at Dewsbury

interesting example from Gilling.* This is the tomb of the founder of Gilling Church, and it is placed in the Church, in the usual position in the chancel, viz., on the north side.

Some misapprehension has existed respecting these monuments with heads, etc., upon them; they have generally been thought to be very rare, whereas they are by no means unfrequent. Again it has been thought that the simple raised cross-slab was gradually developed through these, into the full-length effigy, which is not the case for the full-length effigies are not uncommon at the end of the twelfth century and during the thirteenth, while the crosses with accompanying heads and half-length effigies are most general in the fourteenth century.

Double Coffin Stones at Goosenerg, County of Lancaster.

Cross at Gilling.

The example we give from Hendon,* Yorkshire, exhibits a rare instance of a slab in which the base of the cross is expanded into a canopied niche in which the deceased is represented after a fashion sometimes found in monumental brasses. The two quatrefoils are intended to contain the initials of the deceased.

The following remarks are applicable to both incised and raised cross slabs. Cross slabs are found both in churches and churchyards, and in some positions they have peculiar meanings. Thus the coffin lid of the founder of a church was frequently very significantly placed as the foundation stone of one of the eastern angles of the church. The stone coffin of a founder or benefactor was also frequently placed under an arch in the north chancel wall. It is very usual to find a cross slab as the threshold of one of the church doors, especially of the south door, or of the south porch; denoting the humility of the deceased, or perhaps alluding to the text "I had rather be a doorkeeper in the house of my God, than to dwell in the tents of ungodliness." Some of the stones which we find in this position may very probably have been removed there merely to supply a worn threshold stone; but the instances in which we find them thus are very numerous, and in many cases the stone has all the appearance of being in its original position. In the case of a layman, the foot of the cross is laid towards the east; in that of an ecclesiastic towards the west; for a layman was buried with his face to the altar, a cleric with his face to the people.

It is noticeable that the plain cross is very seldom used upon these monuments, but almost always an ornamented cross. The symbolists considered the plain cross to be the cross of shame, and we very rarely find it used in ancient Gothic work; the floriated cross was the cross of glory, and alluded to the triumph of our blessed Lord, and to our future triumphs and glory through the cross; it is indeed the cross adorned with garlands. Sometimes a smaller circle runs through the limits of the cross, as in the example from Tankersley, and may perhaps be intended to represent the crown of thorns.

Cross at Hendon, Yorkshire.

The amazing variety of pleasing designs which were made from the simple cross or from the combination of the cross and circle, is a good instance of the fertility of invention of the old designers. In the very great number of cross slabs which exist, the instances of the repetition of the same design are very rare.

It may be sometimes rather difficult for an unpractised eye at once to see the cross on some of the complicated designs, but the idea of the cross seems to have been so ever present in the minds of the mediæval Christians that they at once caught at anything which formed even a remote resemblance to the emblem of our faith; in two intersecting roads they saw the cross, and chose these cross roads as places peculiarly suitable for the erection of their village and station crosses; the soldier stuck his sword upright in the earth and its hilt formed the cross before which he prayed.

In the fourteenth century we frequently find the cross beautifully composed of leaves and branches of the vine, in allusion to Christ the true Vine.

The lilies so commonly used in the fifteenth and sixteenth centuries, as terminations to the limits of the cross, were probably in allusion to the Blessed Virgin.

The *steps* or *mound* so very frequently introduced at the base of the cross, were intended to represent Mount Calvary, and are technically called " The Calvary."

Two birds drinking out of a vase or cup is an early Christian emblem; it is found on many slabs in the catacombs. This emblem is strangely travestied in a slab at Bridlington,* where we have a fox and goose drinking out of a vase.

The five wounds. In an example at Kirklees† there are marks or gashes at the four extremities and at the centre of the cross, with drops of blood issuing out of them. These are in allusion to the five wounds in the hands and feet and side of our Saviour

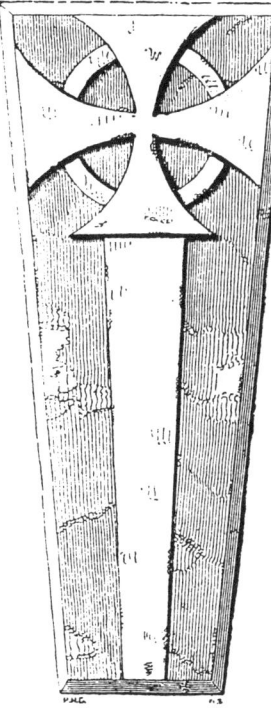

Cross at Tankersley.

Chalice. The symbol of an ecclesiastic. The chalice was placed in the coffin of a Bishop and of a priest; it was also placed in the hand of a deacon, as a kind of investiture, at his ordination, and since no symbol has yet been found on any gravestone, which appears to belong peculiarly to a deacon, the chalice may perhaps have been used as a general symbol of either of the three orders of clergy. An example is found at Jervaulx. The chalice on this stone is of very elegant shape; the sculpture beside it appears to be the letter T, probably the initial

---

* Engraved in the Archœologio Æliance, Vol. II. p. 168.
† Engraved in Gough, Vol. III. pl. 18, p. 247.

of the Christian name of the deceased, who appears by the inscription to have been a canon of St. Leonard's, York. In the second example from Jervaulx, the shape of the lillies here is very unusual. Two steps only to the Calvary, as here, are very uncommon. The inscription is,

hic . iacet in tomba .wills . note callap.
construxit . tabbla . vni . torma vbovena.

Amongst other emblems we may enumerate the following examples, all of which are to be found in Yorkshire.

Cross at Jervaulx.   Cross at Jervaulx.

Pastoral Staff grasped by a hand, a bishop, or abbot, or abbess of which an example is found in Eccleston Priory; *Chalice, Paten, and hand in attitude of benediction*; example, Sproatley. *Chalice and Book*; example, Kirkwood. *Shield*, which may probably denote a knight, example, Goosenerg, Kirk Deighton and Tankersley. *Sword*, generally considered the emblem of a knight, examples, Dewsbury, Thornton, Wycliffe, and Thormanby.

Probably the earliest kind of sepulchral monument in the world was the pillar-stone, a rude unhewn stone set up to mark the place of burial of some great man. These appear to have been used by all primitive nations; many such stones remain in Britain. After the Christian Era, these pillar stones began to be ornamented with a cross or other Christian symbol, either incised or in low relief; sometimes the ornaments were very elaborate as in the example from Hawkswell. In some localities these pillar-stones were in use to a very late date.

In time the upper part of the stone itself was cut into a crucifixion shape, and the pillar stone became the tall sepulchral cross, of which three interesting examples are to be seen in Whalley Churchyard.*

The pillar stone was first modified into the sepulchral cross; the next modification which took place perhaps a century before the Norman Conquest, was into what is usually called the head-cross. This is a stone from one to three feet high, and of different shapes, placed upright at the head of the grave and sometimes accompanied by a smaller stone at the foot of the grave.

These head crosses appear to have come into use (as has been said) about A.D. 950. When the dead was buried in a stone coffin its lid formed his monument; these headstones seem to have been placed over the grave in cases where a coffin of wood or lead, or no coffin at all, was used. They continued in use until the Reformation, soon after which they were again modified into the tall, square, ugly stones, which now crowd and disfigure our churchyards.

Pillar-Stones at Hawkswell.

---

* See Whitaker's History of Whalley.

A BREACH OF PROMISE CASE

FICKLENESS among those whom Eros has smitten is no recent heritage, for our forefathers had their love troubles paraded before the existing authorities of their own times pretty much as breach of promise actions crop up in our assize courts now. So it was with John Wardell, of the parish of Aldborough, near Boroughbridge, in the Archdeaconry of Richmond, and Margaret, daughter of John Kendall, of Markyngton, in the jurisdiction territory and parish of the Collegiate Church of Ripon. As this pair could not settle it themselves—the lady proving obdurate to the ardent attachment of Mr. Wardell, in despair he besought the interposition of the Church, and on the 14th September, 1468, he brought his action which was heard before Christopher Kendall, chaplain of the venerable Collegiate Church of Ripon, and commissary general in the chapter house. There were also present Master John Levesham, clerk and rector of the parish of Esyngton, in the Archdeaconry of Cleveland; William Sawle, chaplain; and Richard Blakett, layman. John Wardell, the plaintiff appeared personally asking for the said Margaret to be adjudicated his lawful wife. Miss Kendall failed to put in an appearance, so the commission was adjourned to the 8th October following, and meanwhile she was cited to appear "in the chapel of the Blessed Virgin Mary in Staynbriggate, Ripon." On that day she obeyed, and John Wardell likewise was present along with Richard Aldburgh, knight; Thomas Paver, chaplain; Richard Greyne, John Kendall, aforesaid " gentielmen "—William Wallworth, Thomas Rute and many

---

*Acts of Chapter of Ripon Cathedral, Surtees Soc., 64.

other neighbouring gentry. The contract was wholly denied by the lady, and the feud being kept up, a Special Commission was appointed for the 20th October before John Levesham, " master, chosen by us in Christ."

This was the final hearing, and after the evidence of both parties had been listened to, the commissary pronounced sentence for the defendant the 23rd November, declaring in somewhat emphatic language that " the said contract was pretentious, worthless, vain, empty and void," thus leaving both parties to marry whom they might please "in the Lord."

Boroughbridge. ALEX. D. H. LEADMAN.

OLD YORKSHIRE PROVERBS

I LIGHTED on a little book one day, in Philadelphia, I had been looking for a good while—" A Dialogue in the Yorkshire Dialect," printed in York in 1684. The vendor asked me five dollars for it, and said it was cheap; and so it was to a bookworm who knew not where to better himself, and I paid my money and got the treasure. It is a dialogue in verse, with a glossary, and the famous pæan " In Praise of Yorkshire Ale," with G. Meritan written on the title-page, as the author, in an antique hand. The scene is laid in the East Riding, on the low lands as I judge, and on a small farm where the tenants have a little more than they can do to make ends meet. But the reason for this lies in a measure within themselves; they are of the kind who have better sinews than brains, and so things go sadly wrong for want of a little more foresight and that power of prevention which is better than cure. So everything on the place is at sixes and sevens, and they are for ever running after their luck. I suppose it is a fair picture of the sort of life your small farmer lived 200 years ago; but there is not a farmer's man now in the West Riding who would tolerate such a life for a week, the discomfort of it, the distraction, or the slavery; and there are but few things in print, so far as I know, that could give one a fairer idea of the progress which has been made among those who have to farm in a small way than such a picture, drawn, no doubt, from the life.

But the best bits of the dialogue to me are the old proverbs which have been handed down from a remoter antiquity, and usually fall from the lips of the farmer with the prefix, "They seay," or "My granny said." He is almost equal to our friend Mrs. Poyser in his command of this mother wit of the people, and would have been a much better farmer if he had put some of it into his day's work, but this does not seem to occur to him; and I have taken out the best of these sayings that your readers may enjoy them, and see at the same time what good things were current in the country-side, when books were rare and newspapers and magazines were not heard of. I shall translate mainly into our modern speech.

"All is well that ends well," is, no doubt, older than Shakespeare; and "Love me leetly love me long," is better as it stands than Charles Reade's version. "The proof of a pudding is in the eating," is still current, as are also these: "God sends the meat and the deil sends the cooks;" "Mare haste warse speed;" "Home's homely if it's never so poor;" "All is not gold that glisters;" I like that word glister. "Over much of a thing is good for nothing;" "Steek the stable door when the steed is stalen;" "While the grass grows the horse starves;" "Hot love is soon cold;" "Proffered things stink;" "Many a little makes a mickle;" "You can have no more of a cat than the skin;" "You may buy a pig in a poke;" "A cat may look at a king;" "Charity begins at home;" "Ill weeds wax fast;" "A tumbling stone gathers no moss;" "A good Jack makes a good Jill;" "Change of pastures makes fat calves;" and "God never sends mouths but he sends meat." This last proverb, however, being always open to the criticism made on it by a poor fellow in Netherdale, when wheat was five pounds per quarter.—"He sends t' mooths to me ha-iver, and t' meet to Robin Stainer."

These proverbs, printed in the time of Charles II., in my little book, and we know not how long before, are still good currency; as is also the saying of the children, "In dockan out nettle," which I also find here. But "Thau's lang a-coming, thou braids of haver malt," belongs to a time when oats were used for beer, as they were to a great extent, I notice, by the monks of Bolton as far back as 1290,—so this proverb is probably dead. "There's no carrion can kill a crow" reminds one of the Scotch proverb, "Hawks winna pike out hawk's een." "Mair the merrier, but fewer the better fair," also belongs to a day when, with all good-will, there might not be enough to go round, but now I suspect the latter half of this is dead. "Meat is mickle but mense is mair" is new to me (by reason of its age), and "As long lives a merry heart as a sad" reminds one of Shakespeare's "A merry heart goes all the way." "That comes in an hour sometimes which comes not in twenty" may have been caught up and brought home by the Crusaders; and "Bragg is a good dog, but he was hanged for biting," differs quite essentially from the modern reading. "Lose a sheep for a haporth o' tar" still lingers in the dales. "As the saw fills the draff sours" reminds me of a proverb I used to hear on the feeding of pigs,

"Fitter leave 'em longing ner loathing," and here is a capital bit well worth preserving :—

"They that eat till they sweat
And work till they're cold,
Such folks are fitter
To hang than to hold."

"Near is my sark, but nearer is my skin."
"As welcome as water in a ship."
"Hungry dogs are fain of dirty puddings."
"An old ape has an old eye."
"A pound of care will not pay an ounce of debt."
"The man falls low who never rises."
"Hope well and have well."
"It's a bad bargain where both sides rue."
"Give a man luck and you may throw him into the sea,"

And "The still saw eats all the meat," are all good; as these are also that look toward the home and the weaker (?) vessel :—

"It's a good horse that never stumbles, and a good wife that never grumbles."
"A grunting wife and a groaning horse never fail."
"They that wed before they're wise will die before they thrive."
"More folk wed than keep good houses."
"What woman but for hope would break her heart?"

So they run, these old proverbs, wise sometimes and witty, or gleaming with a half-savage humour; stinging sometimes like hornets, deep now and then, or tender, or "as goads and as nails."

New York. ROBERT COLLYER.

MOUNT GRACE PRIORY

This fine ruin is in a very lonely situation at the foot of Aincliffe Woods, which clothe for miles the slopes of the western extremity of the Cleveland range. It is in the parish of Ingleby-Arnscliffe, and was anciently a Carthusian monastery, dedicated to the Blessed Virgin and St, Nicholas, having been founded by Thomas de Holland, Duke of Surrey, in the year 1396. The ruins are very extensive, and are the most complete of any of the remains of the Carthusian Order in England. The monastery flourished until the Dissolution, at which time its revenues were valued at £382 5s. 11d. per annum. Henry VIII. granted the site to Sir James Strangeways, Knight, to hold of the King *in capite* by military service. It descended to the Lascelles, and was sold by them to the Mauleverers, and passed by the female line of the latter family to the present proprietor, Douglas Brown, Esq., who takes a great interest in the preservation of the interesting ruins. In a recent paper, published in the *Antiquary*, the well-known archæologist, Mackenzie E. C. Walcott, gave a ground plan of the structure, and an architectural description of the ruins. In a visit made to the Priory by the members of the Cleveland Naturalists' Field Club, during the present session (1881), measurements were taken which showed that Mr. Walcott's plan was wholly unreliable; and the club, therefore, purpose to have the site surveyed and the particulars correctly noted. The Priory is a famous place for trips during the summer season. The nearest station— Welbury—is some four miles distant. The Rev. J. Holme wrote a lengthy poem on the Priory, which was favourably criticised by the press; and Peirson, a Stokesley schoolmaster poet, in a poem on Roseberry Topping, the well-known Yorkshire Parnassus, published in 1783, thus refers to the ruins :—

> Beneath the hills an ancient church appears,
> Its lonely steeple with the ivy clad ;
> Adjoining woods a pleasant horror give,
> The peace is solemn and the site astounds.

The ruins are also the subject of an exhaustive paper in Gordon's *Watering Places of Cleveland;* and in the transactions of the Cleveland Field Club a paper read at one of the meetings, by Mr. W. H. Burnett, is included, and is the most recent contribution to the history and archæology of the buildings, The Carthusian monks were a branch of the Benedictines, one of the strictest and most austere of the religious orders. " They were not allowed to eat flesh, and fasted on bread and water every Friday. They wore a hair cloth next the skin, and walked in their grounds only once a week. At their meals each monk was obliged to eat alone, and to maintain the strictest silence ; and women were on no account permitted to enter the precincts of the Priory. Their beds were of straw, covered with a piece of cloth of the coarsest texture." Only nine houses of this branch of the order were established in England.

THE DEVIL'S ARROW

THESE singular stones stand about a quarter of a mile to the west of Boroughbridge. They are three in number, stand almost due north and south, nearly in a line with each other, the road to Roecliffe passing between the central and southern stones. The north arrow is 18ft. high, 22ft. in circumference, and computed to weigh 36 tons. The central arrow has a height of 21½ feet, is 18ft. in circumference, about 30 tons in weight, and of a square shape. The south arrow is similar in all respects to the central one. All incline slightly to the south-east. They stand about six feet deep in the earth, upon a bed of hard clay, while above that, surrounding them to within a foot of the surface, is a composition of grit, pebbles, clay, and rough stones. Their buried surfaces bear undoubted marks of rough dressing, as if they had been squared with a chisel. Above the ground they are square, while their tops are fluted, but this has been done by the hand of time and the rains of centuries. They are of millstone grit, common enough in many places, but the nearest source of it to this place is Plumpton—eleven miles distant—whence presumably they were brought. Formerly there was a fourth arrow, which stood 7ft. or 8ft. from the centre one. Camden, writing in 1582, says that this "one was lately pulled downe, by some that hoped though in vaine to find treasure." The upper portion of this arrow may be still seen in the grounds of Aldborough Manor, while the lower segment forms part of the foundations of the "Peggy Bridge" in the town of Boroughbridge. What a sacrilege! but "To such base uses may we come at last." The buried portion of the central arrow was laid bare in 1709 by the Rev. E. Morris, then Vicar of Aldborough; and the south arrow was similarly treated in 1876, when the Yorkshire Naturalists' Association visited this neighbourhood. The question may well be asked, "What are they?" Some of the many and various speculations may be of interest. Camden considers "that they were monuments of victory, erected by the Romans hard by the High-street, which went this way." Dr. Stukeley refers them to the Druids, but this is untenable, for these stones bear evidence of dressing with a chisel, whereas the Druids used nought save unhewn stones, unpolluted with a metal tool. Dr. Stillingfleet regards them as "British Deities," erected for worship by our earliest and pagan ancestors; and another speculation is that, as Aldborough in the days of Brigantian greatness was the residence of some of the kings of that tribe, so these stones may be memorials of them. Hargrove, in his "History of Knaresborough," thinks they were the "metæ" around which chariots were turned in the "chariot races." Leland, Drake, Gale, and Lister all agree with Camden in what is the most probably correct opinion—that they are of Roman origin. Their traditional source, as implied by their popular name, is not to be wondered at. They bear no record. History is silent concerning them. So a superstitious people in the dark ages found no difficulty in attributing them, as they did every natural wonder, to the power of that "gentleman" whose attire is "as black as the crow they denominate Jim." The legend runs thus:—The "Old Borough" having excited his wrath, he undertook a mundane journey, with the special intention of improving that offending town off the face of the earth. Standing with one foot on the front and the other on the back of How Hill, some seven or eight miles distant, near Fountains Abbey, he declaimed against the "Old Borough," concluding his oration in genuine Yorkshire :—

> Borobrigg, keep out o' th' way,
> For Auldboro' town
> I will ding down.

He then discharged the bolts from his stone bow—with what success the different positions of the town of Aldborough and the arrows show. But "so the story goes." The obscurity of the origin of the "Arrows" is itself a proof of great antiquity, and all attempts to elucidate it with certainty remain futile. This much is certain, that they are the work of man, and they stand as wondrous monuments to a pristine industry. But they keep their own silent secret, leaving us to still wonder what they mean, whence they came, and who brought them there. Boroughbridge is on a branch of the North Eastern Railway, easy of access from Harrogate and Leeds. In addition to the "Devil's Arrows," there are other antiquities worth visiting, while the scenery and the pure air combine to render it a pleasant day's trip.

Boroughbridge.   A. D. H. L.

AN ANCIENT EAST RIDING HOSPITAL

FLIXTON is a village at the foot of the Wolds, where a hospital was founded in the reign of Athelstan, of which the following account is given in Dugdale's "Monasticon:"—"The charter of the 25th Henry VI. shows that one Achorne, Lord of Flixton, in the parish of Folkton, in the reign of King Athelstan, built this hospital for one alderman and fourteen brothers and sisters at Fixton aforesaid, for the preservation of people travelling that way, that they may not be devoured by wolves and other wild beasts then abounding there, endowing the said hospital with several possessions at Flixton, which were afterwards augmented by other benefactions, and confirmed by the aforesaid King Henry, who also enjoined that, according to ancient custom, the Vicar of Folkton should say solemn mass in the hospital chapel on the Feast of St. Andrew, and after such mass should bless bread and water, and divide and sprinkle it among the people then present, to whom several indulgences were granted by the Popes." There is a certain parcel of land in this vicinity distinguished by the name of Wolf-land, and on the spot where the hospital anciently stood is now a farm-house called Spital.

WITCHES AND WIZARDS.

IF there be one circumstance in the social life of the present generation calculated to stifle a sigh for the return of the good old times so often regretfully spoken of by those whom the bustle of to-day arouses into abnormal activity, it is the fact that witches are extinct. The era of witches was an era extending from dread to confusion. When our little island was so favourably known as "merrie England," doubtless it was eminently deserving of its name in most respects; but even then, in the midst of all its mirth and jollity, a black gloom was spread over the land, oppressive to the souls of the people. That black gloom was of witch influence, horrible, portentous, monstrous, fiendish. The witches were abroad, restless, and uncontrolled in their action and malignity; demons, to encounter whom was sometimes death, always loss and misery. What, then, was the worth of gaiety and ease when the time-wrinkled face, the sunken cheek, and lustreless eye of old age formed a gorgon's head, which froze the blood and harrowed the mind? It was only as the transient stimulant, imbibed to drown a gnawing care which knew no rest and felt no pity; its worth was nothing, or even worse than nothing.

In Yorkshire witchcraft has had a full tide of success. The people seemed born to receive it. Nature gave the county high rugged hills, wild trackless moors, bogs, moist and gloom; and so fitted it to become one of the last earthly resting-places of glamour. The minds of Yorkshiremen are naturally somewhat prone to melancholy and given to wonder. The weird and mysterious have ever found in them a ready place. That fact, I believe, was mainly due to the mountains, and next to the monks. Their religion has never been wholly freed from it. In the sixteenth century Archbishop Grindal lamented that the gentlemen of the county were not " well affected towards godly religion, whilst among the common people many superstitious practices remain." The prelate earnestly endeavoured to root out those practices, but only met with very limited success. The young and the old, the rich and the poor, all clung to the yoke that oppressed them. In 1610 a charm was employed at Skipton Castle to preserve the Earl of Cumberland's cattle from murrain; in 1612 twelve persons were executed at Lancaster for witchcraft; and ten years later another batch of six were executed at York for the same crime. At a still later period the fatal weakness, so far from abating, seemed to have increased. The monster Matthew Hopkins and his assistants received a Government appointment as witch-finders. They were to ply their abominable trade throughout England. They undertook to clear any locality of all its witches for the sum of twenty shillings per victim; and it is needless to state that where wrinkled old beldames were not scarce they drove a very thriving trade. Butler has chronicled the doings of the leader of this illustrious brotherhood :—

> Has not the present Parliament
> A leiger to the devil sent,
> Fully empowered to treat about
> Finding revolted witches out?
> And has he not, within one year,
> Hanged thirteen of 'em in one shire?

Matthew's advent was a terrible visitation, but it certainly had one good effect; it soon reduced witchcraft to a mean and sneaking avocation. The agents of the Government had shown that it was essentially a vulgar thing, born of ignorance and gross credulity, and this humiliation crippled it. It was compelled to desert the castle and the baronial hall, but it found good shelter beneath the thatched roof of the rustic or beside the loom of the weaver, and there it tarried. Its spells were now to be broken not by the agency of gold alone, as in the palmy days; silver was discovered to have an effect it could not resist, and its malignancy became of less awful importance, for when the circle of its influence was narrowed its power was fatally curtailed. The magistrate was now its acknowledged superior. He could punish its practices with impunity, except from itself. And from its persecutor he soon had to become indirectly its protector, for he had often to save the unfortunate crones whom popular madness in the rabid onslaughts of its ignorance and fear would have sacrificed.

The credulity and folly of those who believe in the power of witches are not yet at an end. Horse-shoes are still nailed to stable doors to prevent a raid upon the cattle, and " witch elms " are often planted in the garden of the farm-house to drive witches off the premises. The vulgar yet possess nostrums prescribed by " wise men " and " wise women," in which they place greater confidence than in the prescriptions of the most celebrated physicians. One of the most disgusting of these nostrums is that for the cure of whooping-cough. Despite its loathsomeness it is not discarded even at the present day; forty years ago it had complete supremacy. In 1803 a most respectable surgeon of Leeds, when on a visit to two children who were ill of the cough, saw lying on a table what he thought to be a brace of sparrows, plucked and prepared for cooking. Curious to know the reason for providing such fare, for the circumstances of the parents would allow more generous provision, he asked the mother what she intended to do with the birds. " Birds !" she replied in astonishment; "they are not birds, but mice !" " And what do you intend to do with the mice?" asked the amazed doctor, when he was gravely informed by the mother that she intended to cook them for her sick children, because Mother Shipton's Prophecies recommended this dainty dish as an infallible cure for the tiresome disease his medicines could not conquer.

At the beginning of the century Yorkshire was full of " wise men " and " wise women," though it had only one witch of the old malignant species. Of the " wise," one of the most celebrated, both for personal shrewdness and professional prosperity, was a man who called himself 'Rough Robin of Rumbles Moor." In the savage solitude of this bleak moor the prophet hermit long resided, alternately the joy and consolation or despair of love-sick maidens morbidly anxious for the future. High, however, as was his reputation in the art of depicting future husbands, Robin was even more famed for comprehending the hidden mysteries of the past. Of him the people believed that to ask was to be told; they consequently placed implicit faith in his *dicta*. In 1790 a common carrier, plying between Aldstone and Penrith, had had some goods stolen from his waggon, and in order to discover the thief, he made a pilgrimage to Rombalds Moor to consult the sage, whose fame had reached Cumberland. Robin received the carrier's offering, heard his tale, and dismissed him with the consolatory assurance that if the thief did not restore the stolen property before a given day, it should be the worse for him ! The poor simple dupe departed, overjoyed that Robin had promised so much, never doubting that the goods would be restored. Having arrived at home, he freely circulated the result of his interview among his neighbours; and it happened the report had a wonderfully beneficial effect upon them. Thursday, 25th February, was the day fixed as the ultimate end of forbearance. As it approached, the simple people, seeing that no knowledge of the whereabouts of the goods had as yet been obtained, began to look forward as to a great catastrophe. Would the world be destroyed? Would an earthquake swallow up the offender? Or would some thunderbolt dart down upon him and reduce him to a cinder? They could not tell, but it was better to be prepared for any eventuality. And it is a fact that on the night before the terrible day they loaded the thatched roofs of their cottages with harrows and such implements as would best secure the thatch against a fierce and sudden storm of wind. It was well they did so, for singularly enough a violent hurricane broke out in the night, doing very considerable damage. It was felt in most parts of the kingdom. The eventful morning brought alarm and destruction on every side. Punishment had clearly been meted out, but who was the guilty party? In the indiscriminate wreck none could say, for all had suffered alike. The stolen goods were *not* restored, yet that did not influence Robin's reputation. There can be no doubt that, happening as the storm did in the very nick of time, the recovery of the property was regarded as a mere trifle as compared with the fulfilment of the threat. Nobody could dispute the vigorous execution of Robin's sentence, which they now began to see, did not extend to the actual recovery of the property, but only promised a conditional punishment, which the thief must have received in common with his neighbours.

Robin continued to ply his trade during the rest of his life; but after this great *coup* the solitude of Rombalds Moor was found to exercise too severe an obstacle to the extension of his practice. His fame was now established on every side, and it only remained for him to render himself more accessible in order to reap a golden harvest. So he betook himself into the large towns, where rapid success followed him. In the summer of 1806 he established himself in Leeds, to the horror of the editor of the *Leeds Mercury*, who was at the pains to give him an editorial notice to quit, almost before he had fairly settled. It is certainly most amusing to think how seriously the *Mercury* took the matter of his advent. On the 7th August it informed the sage that "if he did not beat a quick march out of the town he would be before Monday night be tipped with a magic wand called a constable's staff, and lodged in an enchanted castle, where he may confer with his familiars without danger of interruption - except from the turnkey." Such a hint Robin did not fail to take; he left Leeds abruptly no doubt weaving spells to entrammel the monster who had driven him forth.

As a rule, the soothsayers were not malignant. Their vices were mean, but the effects, if troublesome, seldom dangerous. Amongst the most celebrated of these worthies was the Knottingley "wise man," whose reputation was for a long time universal. His wisdom was once very curiously and shrewdly tested, and found to be utterly wanting. An opulent farmer—a man not devoid of humour, but certainly not credulous—had had a cow stolen. He was recommended to apply to the "wise man." Feigning to accept the assurances of his gossips, he consented to apply to the wizard for advice. An opportunity for a good joke at least presented itself. He arose early, and rode into Knottingley on the grey dawn of an autumn morning. The village streets were deserted; the wizard's temple was closed, and showed no signs of occupation. A large and ponderous log of wood, intended for fuel, was lying beside the door, and near it was a bucket of water. These two articles offered the means of perpetrating the joke the inquirer had longed for. He reared the log on end, resting against the door, and placed the bucket of water on the top of it. He then knocked at the wizard's door, who, starting from the bewilderment of sound sleep abruptly broken, demanded " Who's there ? " " Be quick," replied the farmer, " and open the door ; I want to see thee." The wizard, half dressed, opened the door, when down fell the log and the water upon him, both dousing and bruising him. " Oh dear, oh dear ! who's done that ? " moaned the poor wizard, as he scrambled upon his legs. " Na, na ! " roared the farmer, bursting with laughter at the wizard's plight and ignorance ; " if thoo can't tell me who did that, thoo can't tell me who stole my coo ; so good morning." And he hurried away, leaving the poor wretch to meditate upon his disappointment.

Among the prophets two deserve especial mention. Sheffield had one of these worthies, who, when the power of divination descended upon him, abandoned not only the servile habits but also the heathenish names derived from his ancestors, and was henceforth known to fame and the credulous as " the Sheffield tailor." He became the centre of interest in his part of the county by informing the people that the end of the world was fixed for 1805. But although he was by

> Far more skilful with the spheres,
> Than he was with the sieve and shears,

he was only at the best the disciple and imitator of a bolder and more aspiring rogue, George Hey, of Kirkstall, who considered his dignity most fittingly described by the loud-sounding name of " the Kirkstall Prognosticator."

In 1801 it had been revealed to the " Prognosticator " that the end of the world was to arrive in 1806, and George, who to the wisdom of a prophet added the humanity of a true Christian, seeing the iniquity of the thoughtless mass of his fellow-men, determined to raise his voice in an endeavour to recall them from their folly and wickedness. To accomplish his end the more completely he resorted to the newspapers, and the following advertisement appears in many of the journals for October, 1802 :—

To the World at Large.

Repent that ye may be saved ! and live and dwell on the earth for ever in peace with God; for I foretell the length of every man's and woman's life that liveth upon the earth, unless they live for ever and never die ; for on WHITSUN-MONDAY, in the year 1806, it will rain down fire and brimstone until all shall be consumed that know not God ; but all that live in His fear and strive to do His will shall live on the earth for ever. Think not much of me for telling this, for as Noah was the end of the Old World, and beginning of this, so I declare the ending of this world, and the beginning of that which shall follow, and of that there shall be no end. GEORGE HEY.
Kirkstall Forge, near Leeds, Yorkshire, May 2nd, 1801.

The " Sheffield Tailor " could not brook this interference on the part of the Kirkstall man. He soon answered George's advertisement with the announcement that the end of the world would arrive in 1805. The matter was taken up as one of serious import. Although the doctors differed as to the exact time, they agreed as to the result, and their difference was a mere trifle. Whether the end of 1805 or the middle of 1806 was the exact time it mattered but little; the one thing that appeared quite clear to all who hearkened unto the prophets was that it behoved prudent believers to begin to set their houses in order. To complete the effect of these warnings, in October, 1803, the celebrated Johanna Southcote paid a visit to Leeds, where, as indeed throughout all Yorkshire, her followers were numerous. Thanks to the agency of the " Tailor " and the " Prognosticator," and a host of lesser lights, Johanna's disciples believed as sincerely in her marvellous prophecies as ever did good Catholic in the miracles wrought at the shrine of our Lady of Loretto. The object of her visit to Leeds was to encourage the faithful, and to distribute to them the "Celestial Seals," which would protect them from all danger during the approaching period of transition. The seals were to be had, she told them without money, and without price; the only thing wanting to give them full efficacy was faith! Another property of these wonder-working seals was that they would produce patriarchal longevity, and whoever should receive them worthily would—in the opinion at least of the prophetess—live a thousand years. But, alas, it is the fate of all modern prophecy to be be stamped with the character of falsehood. The " Tailor " was first proved to be a false prophet by the mere lapse of time; that, however, did not shake the faith of believers; it strengthened that of the partisans of the " Prognosticator," who triumphed with grim mockery over their rivals. The disciples of the " Prognosticator " awaited the approach of their awful day with deep anxiety indeed, yet with exultation and full confidence in the superior merits of their leader. At length the day came. As a fact its advent was horrible. The sun at his rising looked threatening; the weather was unpleasantly sultry. These were omens which could not be disregarded; even the thoughtless and the scoffer were awed. The faithful were apprehensive, but steadfast. The streets soon became crowded with a restless throng; the air became strongly impregnated with dust, perhaps brimstone! the lurid sun as it sank behind the western hills wore a fiery aspect that drew forth tribulation and woe from the breasts of those who were unprepared to meet the now apparently inevitable doom. Frenzy seized alike upon devotee and scoffer; the tension was intolerable. At last, amid groans and misery, the sun set; the night—" Such night in England ne'er had been, and ne'er again would be"—approached, and passed—as usual. Thus ended this eventful day, adding another to the numerous instances of prophetic delusion for which the beginning of the present century was so peculiarly distinguished. Leeds and its neighbourhood were restored to tranquility by the dawning of the morrow; yet singularly enough, the fame of George Hey was not destroyed either as a prophet in the higher sense of the word, or as a mere fortune-teller, to which he descended.

As a professor of divination of high rank and eminent success, Hannah Green, " the Ling Bob Witch," claims a place in the annals of her kind and the memory of the grateful. Her predecessor, and for some time her rival, was George Mason, the noted astrologer of Calverley Carr, near Bradford. George fell far short of "Ling Bob" both in audacity and success. He certainly amassed a fortune of several hundred pounds; but when he died, in April, 1807, Hannah was in the zenith of a popularity he could never achieve. There is one remarkable incident in the biography of Hannah which seems only to be explained by professional jealousy; and, although it is impossible to say Mason was the cause of it, yet such is the probability. Among the deaths in the *Leeds Mercury* for May 17th, 1806, it is stated that Hannah Green, alias "The Ling Bob Witch," departed this life on Thursday night last, "in her hovel at Yeadon, where thousands of inquisitive maidens have for years resorted to enjoy by anticipation their future destiny." This announcement, so eminently calculated to injure Hannah's connection, was indignantly answered by the sibyl. Next week the editor received the following note, dated Yeadon Moor, May 21st, and signed "Hanner Green"—

"This is to inform Mr. Baines that if he does not contradict my death in next Saturday's paper he must stand to the consequences of the law." "Hanner's" correspondence was not elegant, but it was forcible and free from all oracular ambiguity. It spoke the mind of a determined person, who, having received some injury, was bent upon full reparation. This the editor saw, and to escape the dilemma with as much dignity as possible, his next issue, after denying the death, contains the following exculpatory paragraph:—"Whether we were imposed upon last week by the person who brought us the article announcing the death at Ling-bob, or whether any attempt is now made to mislead us, we have not skill enough in the occult sciences to divine; but the above letter certainly does not appear to be the production of a witch." The editor's error in judgment respecting the origin of the epistle, Hannah was magnanimous enough to treat with contempt; she was satisfied with the explanation. After forty years' practice she at length died in her "hovel" on the 12th May, 1810, and was succeeded by her daughter, Hannah Spence, who inherited her worthy mother's business and a fortune of £1,000—the profits which had accrued therefrom.

In his early life the writer was well acquainted with an old bookseller in Leeds, a man untutored as to school learning, but of vast reading, of considerable mental power and originality of thought, who had been by turns weaver, astrologer, Militiaman, Chartist, philosopher, and poet. His collection of books for sale was large and miscellaneous. His private library was small, but select and choice. It consisted of works on the "Black Art," as he himself described it; and although divination had ceased to be one of his openly acknowledged professions, and although he freely admitted that the whole thing was nonsense, yet such was the influence of his early impressions that he could not resist "casting the planets" of any of his better-known friends or customers at any serious moment in their career.

Leeds. WM. WHEATER.